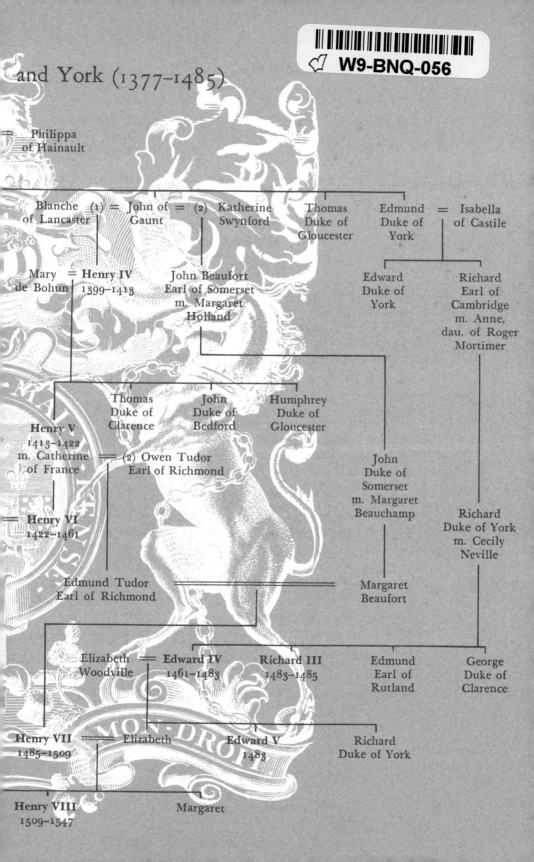

≠ Philippa of Hainault

Blanche (1) = John of = (2) Katherine   Thomas   Edmund = Isabella
of Lancaster | Gaunt   Swynford   Duke of   Duke of   of Castile
                                             Gloucester   York

Mary = Henry IV   John Beaufort   Edward   Richard
de Bohun 1399–1413   Earl of Somerset   Duke of   Earl of
                       m. Margaret   York   Cambridge
                       Holland   m. Anne,
                                                                    dau. of Roger
                                                                    Mortimer

        Thomas   John   Humphrey
        Duke of   Duke of   Duke of
        Clarence   Bedford   Gloucester
Henry V
1413–1422
m. Catherine == (2) Owen Tudor   John
of France   Earl of Richmond   Duke of
                                               Somerset
                                               m. Margaret
== Henry VI   Beauchamp
   1422–1461

                                                            Richard
                                                            Duke of York
                                                            m. Cecily
                                                            Neville

     Edmund Tudor   Margaret
     Earl of Richmond   Beaufort

     Elizabeth = Edward IV   Richard III   Edmund   George
     Woodville   1461–1483   1483–1485   Earl of   Duke of
                                              Rutland   Clarence

Henry VII == Elizabeth   Edward V   Richard
1485–1509   1483   Duke of York

Henry VIII   Margaret
1509–1547

Of Virtue Rare

Of Virtue Rare

Margaret Beaufort,
Matriarch of the House of Tudor

Linda Simon

Houghton Mifflin Company · Boston
1982

Library of Congress Cataloging in Publication Data

Simon, Linda, date
Of virtue rare.

Bibliography: p.
Includes index.
1. Richmond and Derby, Margaret Beaufort, Countess
of, 1441–1509. 2. Great Britain — History — Wars of the
Roses, 1455–1485. 3. Great Britain — History — Henry VII,
1485–1509. 4. Henry VII, King of England, 1457–1509. 5. Tudor, House of.
6. Great Britain — Kings and rulers — Mothers — Biography. I. Title.

DA330.8.R5S55	942	81–6713
ISBN 0–395–31563–8		AACR2

Printed in the United States of America
V 10 9 8 7 6 5 4 3 2 1

Now wel, now wo, now frend, now foo;
    Now lef, now thef, now in, now out;
Now cum, now go, now to, now fro —
    A lord, how gos this world a-bowte!

For Anita McClellan

Contents

Illustrations

Of Virtue Rare

I

The Heiress

IN BEDFORDSHIRE, on the last day of May 1441, a daughter was born to the great-great-grandson of Edward III, John Beaufort, and his wife, Margaret Beauchamp. The child was named for her mother and her paternal grandmother, and the event was delicately inscribed in the family's illuminated Book of Hours.

The infant girl was an heiress of both her parents' fortunes. Margaret Beauchamp had been the widow of a knight when she married Beaufort, and her husband's estates augmented the considerable holdings she already had inherited from her father. John Beaufort had claimed his title of earl of Somerset and with it large estates and important responsibility. He was treated well by the present king, Henry VI, and given positions appropriate to his rank. For years, he had served England in the seemingly endless Hundred Years' War with France. Though his record as a soldier was not startling — he had been taken prisoner in 1421 — the king, in 1443, made him captain general in two strategic areas of France, Aquitaine and Normandy, then still under English control.

For the first two years of her life, Margaret lived at her mother's ancestral home at Bletsoe, Bedfordshire, some sixty miles north of London, with both parents and a constellation of servants making up her small world. As an infant, she was swaddled, each limb wrapped separately in bandages of wool strips about two inches wide. Larger bandages enwrapped her whole body, from toes to neck, in an effort to ensure that her limbs would grow straight and sturdy. She was rocked to sleep in a hand-hewn wooden cradle, suckled for brief periods at frequent intervals to prevent her from gorging herself, bathed carefully and rubbed with oil of almonds or acorns, and, as their only child, was treated tenderly by her parents.

Dark-haired, pale, thin, and somewhat frail, Margaret was bright and alert, with an intelligence evident from the first. With few companions other than the children of visiting nobility, she learned to amuse herself, depend on her own resources, and ask little from those around her. Her world at Bletsoe was comfortable and secure; holidays relieved the tedious routine at the manor, and occasional feasts replaced the usual dinner at midday. When her father traveled to London she shared in the pleasure of the minstrels who joined the entourage to brighten the long and dull medieval journey, fascinated as much by their bright array as by the joyful airs that seemed to linger long after the retinue had disappeared from her sight.

But in April 1443 she saw her father leave on a journey that would last more than just a week or a month. He was going to take his position in France, and one could only guess when he might return. Not understanding the reasons for his departure, the small girl watched as servants gathered his clothing and personal possessions into numerous parcels. He was not there to celebrate her second birthday. By her third birthday, he was dead.

It was only later, long after she had grown from a woman-child into a woman, that Margaret was able to piece together the circumstances of her father's death. Even then, she never knew the truth, for as the years passed, truth and rumor intermingled with myth. Only one thing was sure: John Beaufort was a victim not of battle, but of the pervasive sensibility of war.

He had landed at Cherbourg with some seven thousand troops and began to march through Maine and into Brittany. But his command wavered. He was an arrogant general, refusing to divulge his strategy to his captains. "I will reveal my secret to no one," he told them. "If my shirt knew my secret I would burn it." [1] His captains believed that his "secret" did not exist and that their leader was marching to defeat. He managed to seize one town in Brittany, then returned it for a large cash payment. No one understood that escapade: he was left with neither the town nor the promise of neutrality, which many considered vital in Brittany.

By the following year he returned to England, having made no advances in France. Among the commoners and much of nobility there was a great sense of frustration that one hundred years of war might come to loss for England. Though the king himself, and a small party of supporters, wanted peace more than the crown of France, that peace party was clearly the minority. Most Englishmen could not believe in the increasing strength of French nationalism and the weakness — in morale, in leadership, in physical endurance — of the English soldiers. Victorious leaders were hailed when they returned to London, but any who lost battles and conceded defeat in cities and towns were severely derided.

By the time John Beaufort returned, he found that his reputation had preceded him. He was mocked by his peers and banished from court. Disgraced, he died on May 27, 1444, a probable suicide. At least one poet saw in John Beaufort an example of the "Mutability of Wordly Changes" and commemorated him in verse:

> The noble duke of somersett, John,
> > whome all brytayne and also normandye
> hadde In grett drede (& his enemyes everichon)
> > for in his manhode, puissance, & chevalrye,
> when he was weddyd & In estate most hye
> In the best age (right as hys fortune was)
> > The bull to gronde hym cast cruellye,
> that after soone he dyed: suche was hys grace.[2]

Later, even his daughter could find no evidence of a papal bull that dishonored him, yet rumors circulated that the pope, too, was disgusted with Beaufort's poor service to the king.

Beaufort's death was never spoken of as suicide. At Bletsoe, where his family continued to reside, those who visited the grieving widow alluded only to the strain under which he had worked in France, the weakness of his health before he returned, the epidemics of dysentery and other debilitating illnesses that often swept through the troops. To his family, he died a hero.

John Beaufort left estates in Lincoln, Worcester, Kent, Southampton, Middlesex, Norfolk, Essex, Somerset, Lancaster, Westmoreland, York, Gloucester, Sussex, and Stafford. Though some lands had been bequeathed to his brother, most of his possessions ensured the financial independence of his widow and daughter.

Margaret was raised at Bletsoe under her mother's guidance and given an unusual education for a female at the time. She was taught the obligatory skill of needlework as well as reading, writing, and French. Her tutors remarked on her excellent memory and the speed at which she was able to assimilate material and advance in her studies.

She wanted to learn Greek and Latin, languages reserved for men who would one day join the clergy, but her request was refused. Her mother would not engage a tutor for such esoteric studies. Margaret had no choice but to obey. Years later, she admitted her regret that both languages had been denied to her. She could translate works from French, but it seemed to her that the greatest works were hidden from her in tongues she could not understand.

With no one to share her nursery and then her schoolroom, Margaret withdrew into a world of studies and books. She enjoyed solitude, and her most fulfilling moments were those devoted to scholarship or to religion. Like all young noblewomen of the time, she was duly instructed in the teachings of the church, but unlike most of them, she approached the teachings with an inquiring and receptive mind. Instead of docilely memorizing Christian doctrine, she sought to make it her own and to live by it. Her prayers were not mindless recitations, but fervent communications with a deity in whom she firmly believed and completely trusted. Quiet, introspective, she watched as visitors from the cities and the court came and went at Bletsoe, listened as servants gossiped about a world they could not comprehend, and came to her own conclusions.

When she was eight, her mother married Lionel Welles, one of the king's knights. For widows, remarriage was a sound financial investment, although the wealthy Margaret Beauchamp hardly needed more riches. If a woman outlived her husband — probable, if her husband was destined for combat — she was entitled to a minimum inheritance of her dower, or approximately one third of the man's estate. The more often a woman was widowed and remarried, if she chose her spouses wisely, the more her own wealth increased. Though Lionel Welles would affect his wife's future, he would have very little to do with that of his stepdaughter.

Shortly after John Beaufort's death, Henry VI disposed of Margaret's wardship by assigning a guardian to whom he believed he owed a great favor. Wardships were often extremely lucrative grants, with the guardian receiving ten per cent of the ward's property each year and a substantial payment for the child's marriage. Until the heir came of age, both the land and the person were at the disposal of the guardian.

Margaret, because of her status as an heiress, was a great prize, and she was awarded to a powerful ally of the king, William de la Pole. "We, considering the notable services that oure Cousin therl

4

of Suffolk hath doon unto us and tendering hym therfore the more specially as reson wol, have oure grace and especially propre mocion and mere deliveracion graunted unto hym to have the warde and mariage of the saide Margarete withouten eny thing therfore unto us or oure heires yelding . . ." [3] The king's warrant was sent only days after Beaufort's death. Though left to the care of her mother, Margaret was under the complete control of a man who saw her solely as property, to be held until maturity, and then sold into marriage.

* * *

The earl of Suffolk and his family had risen from prosperous merchants to wealthy barons on profits from generations of war. William de la Pole's father had lent money to Edward III to help finance the war with France, and his sons had fought on battlefields whenever they were called. After William's elder brother was slain during Henry V's attack at Agincourt in 1415, William himself inherited the title and became earl of Suffolk at the age of nineteen. His record as a commander was impressive. At thirty-two he joined the earl of Salisbury in his important campaign against the French.

In the 1420s, when Suffolk sailed for France, he faced a situation very different from that which confronted John Beaufort nearly twenty years later. In the mid 1420s, the French were ready for a leader to raise them from despair. Their political uncertainty rising from the recent death of their king, Charles VI, was compounded by a long series of raids from independent mercenary English armies. These armies, assembled and maintained by one or another of the nobility solely for profit, were illegal but could not be abolished. Their effect on the already demoralized French populace was devastating.

France's prayers were answered in the form of an adolescent girl, Jeanette of Domremy, the daughter of a farmer, Jacques d'Arc, and his wife, Isabelette. Jeanette, or Joan, as she came to be known to the English, heard voices — from angels and from God — that told her the dauphin of France, the heir to the French throne who had been dispossessed in favor of the English king, must be installed to his rightful position. The voices insisted, further, that Joan herself effect that miracle.

The girl left Domremy, gained an audience with the dauphin, and repeated her tale. The dauphin was cautious. He assigned priests and scholars to question her and deliberate. Their investigations took a month. None could find any cause to disbelieve her. God had sent a message through a peasant girl, they concluded, and the French military had only to act.

Meanwhile, the English had begun a siege on an important city, Orléans. One Sunday in October of 1428, English cannon, hurling stones weighing more than one hundred pounds, damaged buildings and mills. Soldiers mined a vital road and demolished a bridge. Exactly a week later, the earl of Salisbury, then in command, was struck by a cannon shot. Half of his face was crushed, one eye completely put out. When he died three days later, Suffolk replaced him.

It was up to Suffolk, then, to deal with the mystical young woman fast advancing on English troops. Joan, despite her claim of communication with supernatural beings, did not awe or frighten the English commander. Life in the fifteenth century provided a fair mixture of the supernatural and the mundane. Ghosts, spirits, angels, and shades did not hover only around uneducated peasants; they figured in the lives of gentlemen and ladies of all rank. Prayer, of course, was a first resort in any momentous decision, but receptive ears awaited an audible reply. Sorcerers could be found in unlikely places: a bored duchess was as prone to magic as a wizened farmer's wife. Like the ancient Greeks, who believed their gods cavorted among them, the medieval English were not surprised that saints would descend to right sinners' wrongs. Suffolk, therefore, dealt with Joan just as he would have handled any opposing commander: he ignored her attempts at diplomacy and assembled his men.

In March, Joan wrote to the English commanders, among whom was "Guillaume de la Poule":

> I call upon you to make submission to the King of Heaven, and to yield into the hands of the Maid, who has been sent hither by God, the King of Heaven, the keyes of all the fair cities which you have seized and ravished in France . . . Most gladly will she make peace with you if you be willing to hearken to her demands, which are that you shall leave France in tranquility and pay what you owe . . .[4]

The English sent no reply to the Maid's letter. Joan had promised that if they did not leave Orléans in peace, "then great misfortune shall fall upon you, which you shall soon remember to your cost." Still, they persisted in campaigning against the city and in proving to themselves that God was on their side.

Finally, on April 29, at eight in the evening, Joan of Arc entered

Orléans, "armed at all points, riding upon a white horse; and she caused her standard to be borne before her, which was likewise white, on which were two angels, holding each a fleur-de-lys in their hands; and on the pennon was painted an annunciation." A procession of nobility met her, "bearing great plenty of torches and making such rejoicing as if they had seen God descend in their midst . . . And there was marvellous crowd and press to touch her or the horse upon which she was." One of the torch bearers pressed too close; Joan's pennon caught fire. The Maid acted quickly, "struck spurs to her horse and turned him right gently towards the pennon and extinguished the fire of it as if she had long served in the wars . . ." [5]

On May 5 she again wrote to the English, this time tying the letter to an arrow and ordering an archer to shoot it to the enemy troops. The English were not moved. No mere child would cause their defeat. Yet the French were profoundly inspired. The girl would lead them to victory, and by the end of May Suffolk's troops were driven from Orléans. On June 12 Suffolk himself was captured; he was held prisoner, ransomed, and at last returned to England. Legend had it that when he surrendered, he said it was to "the bravest woman on earth."

The dauphin was crowned at Rheims in 1429, but he could not save Joan from the fate of a martyr. She was captured by the Burgundians and handed over to the English. Henry's advisers thought it best that the English have nothing to do with a woman so closely bound up with the supernatural, but they had no doubt she must be put to death. They confidently placed her in the hands of French clergy who had long been in English employ. Her inquisitors staged a trial whose outcome had already been firmly decided.

She was kept imprisoned by English guards, a surly group who both hated and feared her and, on orders from her captors, repeatedly tried to rape her in an effort to discredit her claim to virginity. Humiliating examinations, which confirmed that Joan was a virgin, were conducted by matrons and midwives, supervised by the duchess of Bedford. According to rumor, the duke of Bedford was stretched out on the floor above, with his eye to a crack in the slats. Again and again, to establish heresy, the judges questioned her on her wearing of men's clothing, an abomination in the eyes of God. But Joan insisted that it was God's command that she wear men's clothing to carry out the divine instructions. The judges were concerned, too, with her communion with the saints, especially with St. Michael, and

7

wondered if these apparitions were clothed, vibrant, or warm. Did they have a pleasant odor, they asked her. Did she embrace the upper part or the lower part of the spirits? Joan would tell them little: they were true and divine apparitions; that was all she would admit.

The judges intended to prove Joan's impurity, not to bring to light any interior cause for her vision and actions, but their incessant interrogation about sexual matters led future historians to conclude that Joan's repressed sexuality led to hysterical or psychotic behavior. Her contemporaries, however, were not concerned with such analysis. The judges believed that there were three charges, for any of which Joan might be executed: witchcraft, impurity, or heresy. They circled slowly around the accused woman with their mental bludgeons until they realized that only on a charge of heresy could they condemn her. The proof, for them, was her persistent wearing of men's clothing, an act banned by the Church.

On Wednesday, May 30, 1431, as soon as her sentence was read, Joan was taken to the Old Market Place at Rouen, where a fire had already been kindled. An Englishman standing in the crowd was so moved by the sight of the unfortunate young woman that he handed her a small, crude wooden cross. Bearing her gift, Joan was tied to a stake and consumed by flames.

As soon as the news of Joan's death reached England, Henry's armies resumed their campaigns in France. By the end of the year they had gained enough strength to bring the king across the Channel. On Sunday morning, December 16, 1431, ten-year-old King Henry led a procession from the Palais Royal to Notre Dame, followed by a choir. At the cathedral, a long platform had been created for the coronation of the English king of France. Slowly, Henry VI mounted the steps to receive a new crown, treading reverently on a field of deep blue, painted with fleurs-de-lys of gold. The English held feasts and jousts in celebration, but the French did not share their joy.

Though the earl of Suffolk was central in the English defeat by Joan of Arc, his reputation did not immediately suffer. He was, after all, a victim of magic, and his friends believed that once the perpetrator of the magic was dead, the English would surely rally.

Suffolk did not return to France after Joan's death, but remained at court as a trusted adviser and ambassador. Ten years later, however, he again brushed with alleged witchcraft, this time as judge when Eleanor Cobham, the second wife of Humphrey, duke of Gloucester, was accused, along with three accomplices, of mutilating wax effigies of Henry VI in an effort to cause the king's death. Her cohorts were Roger Bolingbroke, said to have been the most famous scholar of astrology and magic at the time; Canon Thomas Southwell, accused of blessing certain of Bolingbroke's instruments; and one Margery Jourdemayne, who, because she resided in the manor of Eye-next-Westminster, was given the chilling sobriquet "The Witch of Eye."

On Sunday, July 23, 1441, Bolingbroke and his equipment were given public display. Among his instruments, besides his conjurer's robe, were four swords with copper images of demons at their heads, and several wax images of the king. The duchess, in her defense, claimed that the wax images were used to attempt to procure her a child by her husband, Gloucester. Jourdemayne was known as a specialist in such matters and allegedly supplied the duchess with aphrodisiacs necessary to ensnare the duke in the first place.

Despite their testimony, the four sorcerers were condemned. Bolingbroke was hanged, then drawn and quartered. Southwell died in prison. Jourdemayne was burned at Smithfield. The duchess, after serving the public penance of walking barefoot through London for three days, was imprisoned for life.

Londoners were not sympathetic toward Eleanor Cobham, who had been Gloucester's mistress before he abandoned his first wife to marry her. They were gratified to see this highborn lady fall so precipitously from her station, and were curious about the events that led to her shame. Much of the information they received came from the many ballads circulated among the populace. In one, "The Lament of the Duchess of Gloucester," Eleanor supposedly tells her own tale of woe.

> "With welth, wele, and worthinesse,
>   I was be-sett on every syde;
> Of glowcestre I was duchesse,
>   Of all men I was magnifyed.
> As lucifer fell downe for pride,
>   So I fell from felicite;
> I had no grace my-self to gwyde —
>   All women may be ware by me.
>
> "Sum tyme I was in riche aray,
>   Ther myght no princes by my pere;
> In clothys of gold and garmentys gay,
>   Me thowght ther was no thyng to dere.
> I purchast fast from yere to yere,

Of poor men I had no pite.
Now ar my wittys all in were —
All women may be ware by me . . .

"All women that ar ware of wark,
My mischeve may ye haf in mynd;
To gef credence to any clerk;
ffor so dyd I, and that I fynd
I wrowght agayne all course of kynd,
And lost my crede for cruelty;
Ther may no blys my balys unbynd —
All women may be ware by me.

"My clerkys callyd up and downe,
All was but mischeve that they ment;
Owre soverayn lord and kyng with crowne
Hym to distroye was owre entent.
All-myghty god omnipotent,
He wyst full well owre cruelte;
Loo, for such marmys I am now schente —
All women may be ware by me."

In the song, Eleanor is duly repentent of her "gret offence" and grateful that she was not executed along with her accomplices. It was punishment enough, she says, to have to give up all that she once enjoyed.

"ffarewell, damaske and clothys of gold,
ffarewell, velwette and clothys in grayne [scarlet],
ffarewell, my clothys so manyfold,
ffarewell, I se yow never agayne;
ffarewell, my lord and soverayne,
ffarewell, it may no bettyr be;
Owre partyng is a privy payne —
All women may be ware by me.

"ffarewell, all mynstralcy and song,
ffarewell, all worldly daliance,
ffarewell, I wote I haf do wrong
And all I wyte mysgoverance.
Now list me nedyr prike ne prawne,
My pride is put to poverte,
That bothe in englond and in fraunce
All women may be ware by me.

"ffarewell, now, all lustinesse;
   All worldly Joy I here forsake;
I am so full of hevynesse,
   I wot not to whom playnt to make.
   But to hym I wyll me take,
      That for us was put upon a tree,
   And in prayers wyll I wache and wake —
   All women may be ware by me." [6]

Though Suffolk, as one of Eleanor's judges, caused her downfall, it was not her own fall that he hoped to effect, but that of her husband, Humphrey of Gloucester. In fact, Eleanor's scandal engendered an atmosphere of suspicion that could not help falling on her husband, and thereby could not help putting Suffolk in a favorable light.

Gloucester had been regent of England for more than twenty years during the long minority of his nephew Henry VI. He had no lack of political enemies; chief among them was Margaret Beaufort's great-uncle Henry Beaufort. Bishop of Winchester since 1406, Henry Beaufort wanted to be pope. Failing that, he aspired to be a cardinal and almost succeeded. He struck up a friendship with Pope Martin V, who offered him the cardinal's hat, but Beaufort's king, Henry V, was adamantly opposed. Beaufort bought influence in government through his indispensable and seemingly bottomless purse. As cardinal, thought the king, he would be uncontrollable. Henry V threatened to rescind Beaufort's bishopric and confiscate all his worldly goods if he dared accept the honor. For once, Beaufort was forced to submit. It may have been the only time.

As chancellor of England, Beaufort would not be cowed by Gloucester, and their enmity was notorious throughout London. Once the archbishop of Canterbury rode eight times between the two to settle a dispute. Throughout the reign of Henry V and well into the reign of his son, Beaufort and Gloucester kept up their noisy public disputes. Finally Beaufort, annoyed at a compromise he was induced to make with his rival, resigned as chancellor of England and sought power in the position he had long coveted: "The Habite, Hatte and dignitie of a Cardinall." [7]

In 1447, Gloucester and Beaufort were still rivals, this time over the conduct of the war with France. Beaufort and his party were calling for peace, even if it meant surrender of English-held land. Gloucester wanted to continue the war. The factions were irreparably divided, and Gloucester, for his strong views, was accused of treason and arrested to await trial. The morning after his arrest he was found dead. He appeared to have suffered "a palsey . . . but all indifferent persons well knewe, that he died of no natural death but of some violent force: some judged hym to be strangled: some affirme, that a hote spitte was put in at his foundement: others write, that he was stiffeled or smoldered betwene twoo fetherbeddes . . ." [8] It appears, however, that the "palsey" was in fact a stroke, brought on in the fifty-six-year-old man by the shock of his sudden arrest and accusation.

Gloucester, too, was the subject of a "Lament" that shows the sympathy he evoked among many Englishmen.

> Compleyne al yngland this goode lordis deth,
>> ffor and ye considre youre causes ben right grete,
> He hath with his wisdom, while hym lasted breth,
>> And with his richesse made the grete gete
>> Of oure enemys to kele, wold they werre or trete;
>> But ageyn mortalite there lith no recure;
>> Now lord, syn no nother remedye may be gete,
>> Have mercy on hym beryed in this sepulure. [9]

Some saw him as Beaufort's victim, fallen at last to the ruthless cardinal. But Beaufort's triumph was short-lived. Two months later, he too was dead.

There was little mourning for Henry Beaufort. As Edward Hall wrote in his obituary, the cardinal was "more noble of blodd than notable in learning; haut in stomacke [strong in courage] and hygh in countenaunce; ryche above mesure of all men, & to fewe liberal; disdaynfull to his kynne and dreadfull to his lovers; preferrynge money before frendshippe; many things beginning and nothing performing. His covertise insaviable, and hope of long lyfe, made hym both to forget God, his Prynce, and hym selfe, in his latter daies." John Baker, his private chaplain, remembered that on his deathbed Beaufort asked: "Why should I dye, having so much ryches [that] if the whole Realme would save my lyfe, I am either by pollicie to get it, or by ryches to bye it? Fye, will not death be hyred, nor will money do nothyng? when my nephew of Bedford died, I thought my selfe halfe up the whele, but when I saw myne other nephew of Gloucester disceased, then I thought my self able to be equale with kinges, and so thought to encrease my treasure in hoope to have worne a tryple Croune. But I se now the worlde faileth me, and so I am deceyved . . ." [10]

In 1447 two men rose to take the place of Beaufort and Gloucester as rivals to each other and for the ear of the king. One was the new heir presumptive to the throne, Richard Plantagenet, duke of York. The other was Henry VI's trusted aide, William de la Pole, earl of Suffolk.

In the 1440s, as Henry's ambassador and as a proponent of the Beaufort peace party, Suffolk was entrusted with arranging a diplomatic truce that would end the war. As Henry had long proposed, the truce would be strengthened by a marriage. It was Suffolk's dream to see the marriage accomplished between his king and Margaret of Anjou.

Margaret was very beautiful. It was said that Henry, on receiving her portrait from France, was immediately taken by her lovely features and glowing youth. Her beauty, however, was of no real importance, nor was her lack of dowry from her then-impoverished father. Henry had to pawn all the crown jewels and household plate for Margaret's trousseau and the articles necessary for the coronation. He presented her with a gold and ruby ring, but even this was not his own. Given to him by his uncle, it was, ominously, the ring Henry had worn at his coronation in Paris at the age of ten, following the execution of Joan of Arc. All that was important to the king at this time, however, was the proposed two-year truce.

* * *

In May, Suffolk stood as Henry's proxy at the betrothal in Anjou and was greeted with acclaim by his welcoming countrymen when he returned to England. But in October 1444, when he arrived in France with his wife to escort Margaret to her new home, he found that additional concessions were demanded. He must agree to surrender Maine and Anjou, or there would be no marriage and no peace. The decision was a wrenching one for Suffolk, but he believed that both the king and the Beaufort faction would back him, and he agreed. In 1425, England had held half of France. With the new agreements, they would lose almost everything.

There was open approval of Suffolk's actions when the duke returned to London, and the king was duly grateful. But at Bletsoe, visitors were less than content with Suffolk's decision and wondered at the motives behind it. At first the talk was quiet and speculative, but gradually feelings became more belligerent. Margaret Beauchamp was concerned, not only for the future of England, but, on a personal level, for the future of her daughter. Young Margaret's fate had been placed in the hands of this powerful magnate, once the confidant of the king but now, five years later, a man fallen into disgrace. By 1450, Suffolk's popularity had plummeted so deeply that he was seen by some as the sole cause of England's downfall in France.

II

A Mervaylous Thyng

Ⅰ N 1450, at nine years of age, Margaret was made more aware
than ever of the uncertainty of fortune, the brevity of fame. Margaret knew that her mother was worried about Suffolk's influence on
her life. She had heard rumors that she would soon be betrothed to
either of two candidates: John de la Pole, Suffolk's seven-year-old
son, or Edmund Tudor, the earl of Richmond, half brother to the
king, nineteen and a soldier for the crown.

Edmund was born from the union of the widow of Henry V,
Catherine, and a certain charming, handsome young Welsh squire
whom Catherine had appointed clerk of her wardrobe. Owen Tudor
came from an important family in Anglesey; his ancestors were de-
picted in the stained glass of a church in Penmynydd. He had fought
heroically at Henry V's side. What attracted Catherine to him was
not his skill as a soldier, not his ancestry, but his lively dancing at a
court fête and his striking good looks.

It was a crime for Welsh and English to intermarry; in 1427, it
was declared illegal, by an act of Parliament, for the queen dowager
to marry anyone without permission of the king's advisers. Nevertheless, by 1430 Owen Tudor and Catherine were married. Despite the
obvious risks, they had three sons and two daughters. Catherine might
have been able to hide her marriage if she had not been so frequently
pregnant, but the king's counselors could not permit such blatant
disregard for their authority.

In 1436 the Tudor children were taken from their mother, and the
queen herself was retired to Bermondsey Abbey. Owen was imprisoned at Newgate, where he eventually charmed a servant and enlisted the aid of a priest to escape. When Catherine died in January

1437, possibly as much from a rapid succession of pregnancies as from her persecution, Owen's fate became even more precarious. Again he was captured and again he escaped, this time to Wales, where he was apparently ignored until 1439, when the king granted his stepfather full pardon.

The Tudor children did not suffer for their parents' indiscretion. They were placed with high-ranking guardians, and two sons, Edmund and Jasper, were valued members of the king's retinue. It was rumored that Henry VI himself preferred Edmund Tudor as a husband for Margaret.

The descendants of Edward III had intermarried and procreated to evolve a complicated family tree. The family of the eldest son had long since died out, but the second son, Lionel, duke of Clarence, had had a larger family, who intermarried with other nobility. His great-granddaughter Anne Mortimer had married Lionel's nephew, the son of his brother Edmund, duke of York. Her sons, therefore, would inherit the York title.

The third son, John of Gaunt, duke of Lancaster, also begat a large family, both legitimate and, until declared legitimate by Parliament, bastards. Henry VI was the last survivor of Gaunt's marriage, but Henry had no children. Unless he produced an heir, the children of Gaunt's mistress, the Beauforts, would carry on the Lancastrian title. With the death of the eldest, John Beaufort, the line was now carried only by Gaunt's granddaughter Margaret.

For many in 1450 the question of inheritance of the crown was not a pressing issue. For Suffolk, however, the question was vital. As a staunch Lancastrian, unwilling to consider the claims of the family of York, he believed that there was only one real heiress. Margaret Beaufort was a potential queen, and if his ward did not claim the crown for herself, she must pass that glorious inheritance to her son.

Suffolk's striving for power had won him great acclaim, but it also proved to be his downfall. Legally, Margaret's fate was still in the hands of William de la Pole. In February 1450, he managed to betroth his son to the Beaufort heiress. The action angered many. Margaret, after all, was no ordinary heiress, and John de la Pole was the son of a man damned by the court. Early in 1450, when public opinion was greatly against him, Suffolk was indicted for several alleged acts of treason. Foremost among them was the accusation that he tried to secure the throne for his son by forcing the marriage with Margaret

Beaufort, "presumyng and pretendyng her to be next inheritable to the corone . . ."

An anonymous poem, "Advice to the Court," warned the king against the villain.

> Suffolk normandy hath swold.
> to get hyt a-guyn he is bold.
>
> Be ware, kyng henre, how thou doos;
> Let no lenger thy traitours do loos —
>   they will never be trewe.
> The traytours are sworn all to-gedere
> To holde fast as they were brether;
>   Let hem drynk as they han brewed.[1]

Suffolk denied his charges, and King Henry, despite the advice of much of the nobility, declared that Suffolk was still "in the kyng's gode grase." But the impeachment created an atmosphere so volatile that Suffolk's presence could not be abided in England. He was exiled for five years. On April 30, 1450, he set out for Dover to sail across the Channel for Calais.

Before he sailed, William de la Pole wrote a farewell letter to his young son:

> I both charge you, and pray you to . . . pass all the great tempests and troubles of this wretched world.
>   And that also . . . ye do nothing for love nor dread of any earthly creature that should displease him . . . Secondly . . . to be true liegeman in heart, in will, in thought, in deed, unto the king our alder most high and dread sovereign lord, to whom both ye and I be so much bound to . . .

He asked his son to obey his mother; to avoid "proud," "covetous," or "flattering" men; to seek wise counsel.

> And last of all, as heartily and as lovingly as ever father blessed his child in earth, I give you the blessing of Our Lord and of me, which of his infinite mercy increase you in all virtue and good living; and that your blood may by his grace from kindred to kindred multiply in this earth to his service, in such wise as after the departing from this wretched world here, ye and they may glorify him eternally among his angels in heaven.[2]

The substance of Suffolk's letter echoed long-sanctioned advice to children. Someday that advice would reappear in the mouth of Polonius. In the mid fifteenth century, it was popularly repeated in one of the most commonly memorized verses of the time, John Lydgate's "Dietary." Besides giving advice for keeping a sound body (covering one's head in winter, eating thoroughly cooked meat), Lydgate offered advice to children for maintaining strong moral character. They were urged to practice temperance in all things and to face life with an ever-cheerful countenance.

> Meke in troubill, glad in poverte,
>   Ryche with litell, content with suffisaunce,
> Never grucchyng, but mery lyke thy degre;
>   Yf physike lakke, make this thy governaunce.
>
> To every tale, sonn, gyff not credence;
>   Be not hasty nor sodenly vengeabill,
> To poure folke do no violence,
>   Curteys of langage; of fedying mesurabyll,
>   On sondry metis not gredy at the tabill,
>   In feding gentill; prudent in daliaunce;
>   Close of tunge, of worde not deceyvabill,
>   To set the best sette al-wey thy plesaunce.
>
> Be clenly clad aftyr thyne estate;
>   Passe not thy bondys, kepe thy promise blyve;
> With thre folkes be not at debate —
>   ffirst with thy bettir beward for to strive,
> A-geyne thy felawe no quarell do contrive,
>   With thy soget to strive it were shame;
> Wherfor I counsell pursue all thy lyve
>   To lyve in pease and get the a good name.

Lydgate added advice that Suffolk knew too well:

> In youthe be lusty, sad whanne thou art olde —
> No worldely Joye last but A whyle . . .[3]

On May 1, 1450, Suffolk sailed from Dover. Not far off the coast, his boat was intercepted by another, the *Nicholas of the Tower,* and Suffolk was summoned on board. As soon as he was told the name of the ship, he knew he was a doomed man. He once had been told a prophecy: only if he escaped the danger of the Tower would he be safe.

He was allowed time to be shriven. Then, on May 2, he was rowed out to sea in a smaller boat with a gruff Irish companion. There, with a rusty sword, his head was cut off by six hacks of the dull blade. His body was brought back to Dover and thrown on the sands.

By May 5, the shocking news had already reached London. William Lomnor wrote to his friend John Paston, giving as many details as he had been able to learn. He was "right sory of that I shalle sey, and have soo wesshe this litel bille with sorwfulle terys that on ethcs ye shulle reede it." The grim events were related, including the small consolation that Suffolk may have had his confessor with him. Lomnor added that after the duke was dead, his "gown of russette and his dobelette of velvet" were stripped from him and "his hedde was sette oon a pole" near his body. "Whatte shalbe doo forthere I wotte notte," Lomnor wrote, "but thus fer is yt . . ." [4]

When the king received news of the gruesome execution, he ordered the body retrieved and buried. Suffolk's supporters were horrified, and, despite their efforts, the identity of the executioners was never discovered. But the *Nicholas of the Tower* was a royal ship. It could not have been ordered to sea except by someone of the high nobility. It may have been the king himself, convinced at last by Suffolk's rivals that the duke was a horrendous traitor. Or, as rumor had it, it may have been the strongest of those rivals, the son of Anne Mortimer, Richard of York.

* * *

Suffolk's death, however shocking it was for the inhabitants at Bletsoe, liberated Margaret from her bond to John de la Pole. Too important an heiress to be relegated to the son of a disgraced man, she found herself once more handed as a prize to worthy allies of the king. This time, the profitable guardianship was awarded to Edmund and Jasper Tudor.

Henry VI's affection for his two half brothers seems to have been genuine, but his presentation to them of earldoms — Edmund of Richmond, Jasper of Pembroke — was also politically astute. Henry had only a weak identification with Wales because of his father's birth there, and he felt he needed a stronger presence to mitigate political unrest. Welshmen had long suffered legal discrimination by the English. Penal codes provided that Welshmen could not acquire property within or near the English boroughs; they could not serve on juries; could not marry English citizens; could not hold office. No Englishman could be convicted on the oath of a Welshman. For most Englishmen, Wales was a vast unknown territory inhabited by barbarians. In fact, the king's writ was largely ignored there, replaced by a government of powerful lords. Wales had its own courts, taxes, civil and military authority — all obstacles to the rule of the king.

But the Tudors, through their father, were half-Welsh, and both were popular ambassadors for Henry in their homeland. In return for their loyalty and good faith, Henry gave them Margaret Beaufort. Because Margaret was eleven, her marriage to John de la Pole could be considered void. Girls older than twelve and boys older than fourteen were bound legally to their marriage agreements.

She had ardently wished to be freed from the attachment to John de la Pole. Much later, she completely denied the betrothal by perpetrating a legend about her marriage that revealed her own desire. She claimed that she herself had been obliged to choose between Suffolk's son and Edmund Tudor, and at first could not decide. She asked one of her servants, "an old Gentlewoman whom she moche loved and trusted, which dyd advyse her to commend her self to St Nycholas the Patron and helper of all true maydens, and to beseche him to put in her mynde what she were best to do."

Margaret had prayed by day and especially by night for guidance. Finally, "a mervaylous thyng" occurred:

> As she lay in Prayer calling upon St Nycholas, whether slepynge or wakeynge she could not assure, but about four of the clocke in the mornynge one appered unto her arrayed like a byshop and naming unto her Edmonde had take hyme unto her Husbande. And so by this meane she dyd encline her mynde unto Edmonde, the Kyng's Broder . . .[5]

Although by convention children were capable of consent from the age of seven, Margaret's vision was no more marvelous than the prospect that a powerful guardian would allow a nine-year-old heiress to refuse to marry his own son. The apocryphal tale does, however, reveal Margaret's deep desire to have control over her own life and her total faith in the efficacy of prayer. In 1455 she was married to Edmund Tudor. This final union with Edmund was twice blessed: by the king and by God.

The ward became a wife and accompanied her husband to Pembroke Castle, the Tudor-family stronghold, owned by her brother-in-law, Jasper. She exchanged central England, with its access to London and its flow of court visitors, for the wild and desolate region of South Wales.

Pembroke was a stony and imposing fortress built high on a rocky mound, with a twelfth-century round keep rising eighty feet and extending outward fifty-four feet. A drawbridge connected a forebuilding to the second story of the keep; there, seemingly endless spiral staircases let out onto each of the four stories. The living quarters were in a separate inner bailey near the keep. Everything about the castle was cold and forbidding. The stones were immense; the walls, thick and impenetrable. Footsteps echoed through the huge bare halls.

Edmund was soon sent to battle to settle what seemed to be a local skirmish among some Welshmen and then developed into nearly open rebellion. Jasper fought at his brother's side. For months, Margaret was alone at Pembroke. She knew no Welsh, the language of her servants. Often she would withdraw to her own apartment with her books.

Her childhood, however, had prepared her for loneliness. Always given more to study and prayer than to whatever gaiety aristocratic life might offer, Margaret did not suffer in isolation. At fourteen, the thin, dark-haired, quiet girl could do no more than accept her fate. She had been obedient and respectful as a daughter; she had been outwardly docile as a ward; she would be, as expected of her, an exemplary wife.

By her fifteenth birthday, Margaret was pregnant. Midwives were probably summoned immediately to advise her about her health during pregnancy, the first time such information was ever imparted to her. She was told what symptoms were normal and was cautioned that certain signs meant that she or her unborn child might be in peril. Diet was of special concern; she was advised to eat light, small meals, avoiding fatty meats and heavy gravies. She must avoid rice, chestnuts, sour fruits, spices, and lard because they would cause constipation. Should she become constipated, she was to eat apples fried with sugar, especially beneficial if taken on an empty stomach at breakfast, followed by good wine or apple juice. Figs, morning and night, would also help "lose the belly." If dietary methods failed, she could always resort to an enema of chicken soup, sugar, and salt. If she had been a peasant woman, she was warned, she would have to make do with water in which mallows or hollyhock had been steeped. If even an enema did not help, she might try a suppository of soap, lard, or egg yolk.

Physicians were never consulted for pregnancy, and Margaret knew that when she was confined for delivery, only women would be allowed to attend to her. As late as 1522, a German physician with insatiable curiosity dressed as a woman to observe a birth. His trespass was punished: he was burned to death. There was no training offered to midwives other than experience and methods handed down from generation to generation. Written instruction was thought to be shameful; the intimate matters of women might then become known to men, causing them "the more to abhore and loath the company of women." [6]

Much of midwifery had remained unchanged from the time of Soranus, a second-century Greek physician who practiced in Alexandria and in Rome. He advised every midwife to have clean hands and trimmed and rounded fingernails, since she would have to insert her index finger (covered with grease, oil of almonds, or oil of white lilies) into the laboring woman's vagina to determine the dilation of the cervix, and after delivery would again have to insert her finger to remove any blood clots that might adhere to the uterine cavity.

He trained midwives to look for certain signs during the pregnancy that would indicate the presence of disease or the possibility of stillbirth or miscarriage. These signs were well known to the women who attended Margaret, and they watched her carefully, not sure that such a small and frail young woman could produce a healthy child — and survive.

They examined her breasts for slackness, which they believed indicated a potential stillbirth. They questioned her about her diet: Did she crave foods "which be against nature, and not wont to be eaten or drunken?" Did she have frequent nightmares? Did she have a "stinking and filthy" vaginal discharge? Did she feel pain "about the secret parts?" Had her belly suddenly become cold?

They noted her eyes: Were they ringed and hollow? They watched for extreme pallor or sudden deep swarthiness. They smelled her breath, certain that a bad odor meant a miscarriage would occur in two or three days. From time to time, they would place their hands in very warm water, then lay them on Margaret's belly, waiting for the fetus to stir. If "the child stirre not, is a sign that it is dead." [7]

Though Margaret was pale, tired, and often uncomfortable, the midwives saw no signs of any problems and believed that she would bear a healthy baby. But in November, when Margaret was just completing her sixth month, she suffered a terrible shock that sent the midwives hurrying to her in alarm.

Edmund had been in battle again for the king, when suddenly he fell ill. He was brought to the nearest fortress, Carmarthen Castle, treated, but failed to recover. On November 3, he died. When word reached Pembroke Castle, Margaret was desolate, but her sorrow did not show itself in the wild grief the midwives feared would bring on a miscarriage. Instead, Margaret turned to prayer for consolation, showing once more the emotional self-sufficiency that had characterized her youth. She prayed for Edmund's soul; she prayed for herself; and she prayed most intensely for her unborn child.

November was bleak and chilly; December, hardly brightened by holiday feasts. At last, on January 28, 1457, midwives hurried along the passage to Margaret's chamber, carrying with them the few items necessary to aid the birth of her child.

The pain was frightening, but the midwives' comfort and encouragement alleviated some of the fear. Margaret refused offerings of food and drink, grateful for the fire that the women kept stoked and that warmed the drafty room. The women were closely attentive to Margaret, noting her contractions and discussing among themselves whether or not some pepper should be placed beneath her nose to provoke her into a fit of sneezing, thereby speeding labor. Ideally, the midwives thought, labor should be brief: "twenty pangs or within those twenty." [8] But rarely was that ideal realized.

The midwives stroked her belly and kept ready a special girdle thought efficacious in aiding delivery. They taught her when to hold her breath, and they often prayed, clutching an amulet they thought would help ease the terrible pain that racked the thin body of the young widow. They also readied a small "birthing stool" or "short, narrow, high-standing bed" [9] on which Margaret would be placed if it appeared that her child would be born in one of sixteen "unnatural" positions. A supply of cloths was held at the back of the stool, in easy reach of the midwife. Her hands were slick with oil in case she would have to turn the child in the womb to prevent a breech birth. If only one foot protruded, she would have to lift Margaret up at her thighs, then attempt to turn the infant to a head-first position. The midwife knew this was a difficult procedure, one that often failed. If it did, she would have to pull out the child gently in whatever position it appeared.

Anxiously, she watched, certain that this child would present itself head first, but uncertain whether it would be healthy or whether it would live. Like most midwives attending noblewomen, she had been licensed by a bishop to empower her to baptize the infant if it appeared that the newborn might soon die.

Margaret's child, however, did not die. Though her son was small and frail, he was healthy. Immediately, he was taken from his mother, washed, and anointed with oil of acorn. His umbilical cord was cut and tied about two inches from the navel. When it dried and fell off, a powder of burned calves' ashes or snail shells would be applied to the navel.

The navel itself was examined closely. It was believed that if the navel protruded, with no wrinkles, the mother would thereafter be barren. If there were wrinkles, the number would forecast how many children the mother would yet have. If the wrinkles were close together, future pregnancies would be close together; if far apart, a few years might intervene between each pregnancy.

The infant was handled gently. His nostrils were cleaned out, and he was held down to allow him to cough up any substance in his throat. He was quickly swaddled.

Perhaps Margaret followed the prescription of the time and nursed her son. She may, however, have chosen to hire a wet nurse, a local woman of sound health and ruddy complexion, who would abstain from onions, garlic, vinegar, pepper, too much salt, and sex. "Love's intercourse she must shun — or else go in for it very moderately" to avoid another pregnancy.[10] Though her remuneration was not grand, the wet nurse was assured of an adequate diet of white bread, meat, vegetables, and good wine. She was freed from any additional work lest the strain diminish her supply of milk.

While the newborn was being cared for, the midwife attended to Margaret. A linen pad had been placed beneath the perineum as the infant was emerging, and now the tear was washed with butter and wine, pressed together, and sewn with silk threads. The stitches were then covered by a clean linen pad that would be changed daily for a week.

Despite the pain and exhaustion, Margaret felt a great infusion of emotional strength at having produced a living child, a son. More than her marriage, more even than the death of her husband, this event marked the boundary between childhood and womanhood. No longer did she feel that she could not control her fate: now she would direct her own life and that of her child.

When her Tudor relatives visited her in congratulation, they urged her to name her son for his grandfather and in honor of his Welsh heritage. But Margaret had decided on another name. She would not name the child Owen. She would not call him Edmund. Instead, she insisted that the boy be called Henry: a good English name, she thought; the name of kings.

III

Murdre & Much Pride

T HE EVENTS of Margaret's short life made her realize fully that her son had been born into a world of dissension and violence. The Hundred Years' War, which had blighted her own childhood and youth, finally was ended, but new fighting, this time domestic, had begun. This overblown internecine conflict involved two families of the descendants of Edward III, long rivals, the Houses of Lancaster and York. From 1455 to 1485, England would suffer as the two sides struggled for power, each trying to wrest and secure the crown of England. Years later, the battles were designated, romantically, the Wars of the Roses: the white rose from the badge of the House of York; the red rose, of Lancaster. If that elegant flower masks the brutality of the age, no epithet could be less apt.

Fluted armor, newly imported from Italy, was taken up with enthusiasm because of its ability to deflect arrows, swords, and spears. Those weapons gave way to maces and flails; bludgeoning became a favored means of combat. Though the heavily armored men could fight for only a few hours, the fighting was intense and savage. Hostilities went beyond the battlefields.

English society became violent and convulsive. The anger and distrust that permeated the aristocracy filtered down to the populace. Murder became an accepted means of resolving disputes. The "Wild Welshmen" who fought for the Lancastrians, the Yorkshire peasants who rallied behind Richard of York, knew little of their particular moment in history but had learned well the art of ambush and massacre. Soldiers returned to their fields with arms and quick tempers.

At the time of her son's birth, Margaret knew that neither she nor the child was in direct danger. Henry VI, the Lancastrian heir, was still king, and after eight years of marriage to Margaret of Anjou he at last had a son. But if the Yorkists succeeded in usurping the throne, if both the king and his heir were killed, Margaret and Henry Tudor would be in great peril. News came slowly to Pembroke, and from word of the first confrontation Margaret never relaxed her vigilance and never forgot her prayers.

* * *

The white rose was borne by Richard, duke of York. York, "perceiving the king to be no ruler, but the whole burthen of the realme to reste in direction of the queene ... began secretlie to allure his friends of the nobilitie; and privilie declared unto them his title and right to the crowne, and likewise did he to certaine wise governours of diverse cities and townes. Which attempt was so politikelie handled and so secretlie kept, that provision to his purpose was readie, before his purpose was openlie published." [1]

York's intrigue was greatly aided by the general antipathy of the populace toward Margaret of Anjou. Though her marriage to Henry VI had at first been hailed as an English victory, there had been major territorial concessions for the marriage and peace. It had soon become apparent that England had gained nothing and lost much when the French princess wed the king.

Eight years of marriage had made Margaret a disillusioned woman. She was described by the chronicler Holinshed as "a woman of great witte, and yet of no greater wytte than of haute stomacke ... desirous of glory and covetous of honor; and of reason, pollicye, counsaill, and other giftes and talentes of nature belongyng to a man, full and flowyng of witte and wilinesse she lacked nothing, nor of diligence, studie, and businesse she was not unexperte; but yet she had one poynt of a very woman, for, often tyme, when she was vehement and fully bente in a matter, she was sodainly, like a wethercocke, mutable and turnyng." [2] Though her emblem was a daisy and her badge a white swan, Margaret of Anjou was seen not as an example of femininity but as a ruthless, strident, and temperamental virago. One poet, writing in the 1460s, went so far as to suggest that all of the king's troubles came from his marriage.

> I wedded a wyf at my devyse,
>   That was the cause of all my mon . . .
> Sum tyme I roode in clothe of gold so red,
>   Thorow-oute ynglond in many a town;

> Alas, I dare nowth schewe now my hede —
> Thys world ys turned clene uppe so down! [3]

In 1453 the king fell ill with a mysterious and still-inexplicable malady. Completely withdrawn from the world, Henry sat motionless, his eyes downcast, unable to speak or acknowledge any communication. The queen acted decisively.

> Item, the Queene hathe made a bille of five articles desiryng those articles to be graunted; wherof the first is that she desireth to have the hole reule of this land; the second is that she may make the Chauncellor, the Tresorere, the Prive Seelle, and all other officers of this land, with shrieves and all other officers that the Kyng shuld make; the third is, that she may yeve all the bisshopriches of this land, and alle other benefices longyng to the kynges yift; the iiijth is that she may have suffisant lyvelode assigned hir . . . But as for the vth article, I kan not yit knowe what it is. [4]

Margaret of Anjou was determined to exercise her rights as queen of England. "The Quene is a grete and strong laboured woman, for she spareth noo peyne to sue hire thinges to an intent and conclusion to hir power." [5] But the rule of the land did not go to Margaret; instead, events favored a man she distrusted and despised: the ambitious Richard of York. Margaret's wrath was intense. Yet she could not change Parliament's decision.

The queen almost despaired over maintaining her own position. Her desperation became even more profound in October 1453, when at last she presented Henry VI with a child. With her husband still in his trancelike state, she alone took responsibility for naming the heir. As Margaret Beaufort would do four years later, she gave her son the name of an English king — but not that of her husband. She called the infant prince Edward.

The child was brought to his father by the duke of Buckingham, but Henry made no response. Then Margaret broke in, took her son in her arms, and thrust him before the unseeing eyes of the king, pleading with him to bless the child. "But all their labour was in veyne, for they departed thens without any answere or countenaunce savyng only that ones he loked on the Prince and caste doune his eyene ayen, without any more." [6]

The birth of the child spurred Margaret's ambitions and threatened to thwart York's. The heir stood between him and the throne, even if he succeeded in overthrowing the king. York knew, however, that many would not sanction another reign by a minor, remembering the dissension among those who had attempted to rule in Henry VI's name for twenty years. York used his protectorate to gather strength and support for his faction.

In January 1455, Henry recovered as suddenly as he had fallen ill.

> Blessid be God, the Kyng is wel amendid, and hath ben syn Cristemesday; and on Seint Joncs Day commaunded his awmener to ride to Caunterbury with his offryng, and commaunded the secretarie to offre at Seint Edward. And on the Moneday after noon the Queen come to him and brought my lord Prince with here; and then he askid what the princes name was, and the Queen told him Edward; and then he hild up his handes and thanked God therof. And he said he never knew him til that tyme, nor wist not what was seid to him, nor wist not where he had be whils he hath be seke til now. And he askid who was the godfaders, and the Queen told him; and he was wel apaid.[7]

Word that the king had regained his sanity spread quickly. Margaret Beaufort and her family were relieved both of their anxiety about the king and their concern about retaining Lancastrian rule. But they were aware that the government had weakened during Henry's illness. York had become especially angry with Margaret's uncle Edmund Beaufort, duke of Somerset. Somerset had long been in the king's favor, but during York's protectorate, York himself had taken over the government of Calais from the duke, charging him with unconscionable conduct, for which he was imprisoned. Henry was quick to release his aide and kinsman, and pardoned him, but felt it necessary to strike a compromise with York by fining both men. This was an attempt to reconcile what he saw as mere political rivalry.

Margaret Beaufort, learning of the incident from those close to her uncle, probably thought the king naïve. York was evidently intent on proving that Somerset and other Lancastrians in the king's retinue were no less than traitors. He had the support of two noblemen — the earl of Salisbury and the earl of Warwick — and many believed he was in command of sizable troops. It was probably no surprise to Margaret when she heard that York had presented Henry with a letter of ultimatum: "We wyll not now cesse for noon such promysse, surete, ne other, tyl we have hem wych han deserved deth, or elles we to dye there fore."

In a rare show of strength, Henry replied that he could judge the Yorkist traitors for himself. "I shall destrye them every moder sone, and they be hanged, and drawen, and quartered, that may be taken afterward, of them to have ensample to all such traytours to be war to make ony such rysyng of peple withinne my lond . . ." [8]

On Thursday, May 22, 1455, in a field near the Abbey of St. Albans, York and his men confronted the king and his army. The exchange of letters pointed to one end only.

> Rather then they shall have only Lorde here with me at this tyme [wrote Henry], I shall this day, for her sake, and in this quarrell my sylff lyve or dye.

York replied:

> The kyng . . . will not be reformed at our besechyng ne prayer, ne wylle not understonde the entent that we be comen heder and assembled fore and gadered at this tyme; but only ys full purpose, and there noon other wey but that he wole with all his power pursue us, and yf ben taken, to geve us a shameful deth, losyng our lyvelode and goodes, and our heyres shamed for evere. And ther fore . . . better yt ys for us to dye in the feld then cowardly to be put to a grete rebuke and asshamefful deth; more over, consederyng yn what peryle Inglonde stondes inne at thys owre, therefore every man help . . . to redresse the myscheff that no regneth, and to quyte us lyke me in this querell.[9]

Neither side believed itself to have any choice. Each side believed it was fighting for the survival of the country. The battle of St. Albans stands as the first in the long feud between the roses.

The Lancastrians were outnumbered. Some said three thousand assembled with Henry against five thousand with York. But the battle was won more by strategy than by number. The earl of Warwick broke the king's ranks with a strong assault and blockaded the town's marketplace. Four in the king's bodyguard were killed by arrows, and Henry himself was slightly wounded in the shoulder. When the Lancastrians fled, defeated, Henry was given sanctuary in the abbey.

Casualties were few, considering the number of soldiers involved. Perhaps sixty died — and among them was the duke of Somerset, Margaret Beaufort's uncle and the man York most hated. After the battle, York, Salisbury, and Warwick came to the king and knelt humbly before him. Their mission, they said, was solely to oust traitors from the king's council. They begged for forgiveness. And Henry forgave them. York was made constable of England; Warwick was awarded Edmund Beaufort's post in Calais.

But York was ambitious for greater power than that of constable. He did not disband his followers, was seen almost constantly in armor, and began to assemble a battery of weapons. Nevertheless, despite his antipathy to the Lancastrians, when Henry again lapsed into a state of mental collapse in October 1455, York was again named protector by Parliament.

This time he insisted not only on more power but on greater remuneration. His call for more money probably reflected a grievance against the king for sums owed him for his service in France, large sums that had not been paid, although Edmund Beaufort received his promised fees. He also insisted that his protectorate continue after Henry regained his sanity: Parliament alone would decide when he could be dismissed. The last provision led many to believe that the duke planned to assemble considerable Yorkist support in Parliament.

Predictably, the queen was incensed by York's new accession to power, but she could do nothing except try to rally supporters to her own cause. Among the strongest were Edmund and Jasper Tudor, and it was while in the queen's service in Wales, in fact, that Edmund fell ill and died. Margaret of Anjou's supporters, however loyal, could not equal the Yorkist strength. When Henry regained his sanity early in 1456, he acceded to the duke's demands by appointing him chief councilor. The queen vehemently opposed her husband's display of weakness and left the court in anger, withdrawing with her young son to the palace at Greenwich. There she established a court of her own and conferred with trusted advisers about strategy for ousting York and his men from the king's government.

Margaret, as queen, had the power to assemble an army and direct it to battle. The peculiar character of the Wars of the Roses came not only from the independent military powers of the king and queen, but from the power of any nobleman to hire and maintain a private army to do his bidding. Such armies were ubiquitous in England during the fourteenth and most of the fifteenth centuries. They were possible because of the curious practices of livery and maintenance, which resulted in the proliferation of what were, in effect, adult gangs.

Livery and maintenance provided for the hiring of mercenaries, who would be given a badge, sign, or costume associated with one or another of the noblemen. The badge might come from the family's coat of arms, like the *planta genesta* of York or the white swan of Margaret of Anjou or the portcullis of the Beauforts. Once these mercenaries were under contract, they were maintained by the lord to fight for any grievance or cause that he deemed worthy of battle, raid, pillage, or even merely a procession to show force.

The practices had long been discouraged and even outlawed by generations of rulers. In reality, private armies flourished, and nobles believed themselves powerless and vulnerable without their aides. Over a hundred years earlier, in 1327, Edward III had sent out an edict prohibiting his peers from maintaining armies: "Because the king desires that common right be administered to all, to rich as well as to poor, he commands and forbids that any of his councillors or of his household or any of his other ministers or any great man of the realm, by himself or through another . . . shall take upon them to maintain quarrels or parties in the country, to the disturbance of the common law." [10]

Again in 1390, Edward III's nephew Richard II had found himself dealing with the same problem. Instead of advising only his peers of his prohibition, he had included clergy as well:

> Whereas by the laws and customs of our realm, which we are bound, by the oath made at our coronation, to preserve, all our lieges within the same realm, as well poor as rich, ought freely to sue, defend, receive and have Justice and Right, and the accomplishment and execution thereof, in any our courts whatsoever and elsewhere, without being disturbed or oppressed by maintenance, menace, or in any other manner . . . We have ordained and strictly forbidden by the advice of our great council that no prelate nor other man of Holy Church nor bachelor nor esquire nor other of less estate give any manner of such livery, called livery of company to knight or esquire if he is not retained with him for the term of his life, for peace and for war, by indenture, without fraud or evil device, or unless he be a domestic and familiar, abiding in his household . . . And that none of our lieges, great nor small, or what condition or estate he be, whether he be of the retinue of any lord or other person whatever who belongeth not to any retinue shall not undertake any quarrel other than his own, nor shall maintain it, by himself nor by other, privily nor apertly.[11]

Richard had called for the removal of all livery within ten days of his proclamation. His edict was largely ignored.

Interestingly, Richard differentiated between livery and maintenance and indenture, which was the means by which the king himself recruited soldiers. Contracts were made with commanding officers for a certain number of troops to be delivered up to the king when necessary. The officers, in turn, made a contract with each soldier, stipulating the term of the agreement and the fees involved. The contract was inscribed, in duplicate, on a piece of parchment, which was then cut in an irregular pattern between the two inscriptions so that each half matched only the other and no other contract. The toothed pattern gave the contract its name: indentures.[12] While indentures would enable a nobleman to recruit his own army, the caliber of soldier would be far different from that assembled by livery and maintenance. Indenture tended to produce a retinue of professional soldiers; livery and maintenance gave rise to rowdy rabble.

Now, in 1461, Henry VI confronted the problem again:

> No lord, spiritual or temporal, shall from henceforth give any livery or cognisance, mark or token of company, except at such times when he has a special command from the king to raise people for the king's aid, to resist his enemies, or to repress riots within his land ... Also, that no lord ... shall knowingly receive, keep in his household or maintain thieves, robbers, oppressors of the people, those guilty of manslaughter, ravishers of women, and other open and notorious perpetrators of misdeeds, against the law ... upon penalty of the king's great displeasure and the perils that may ensue therefrom.[13]

Henry's proclamation was disregarded, as those of his predecessors had been. The practice of livery and maintenance had served the nobility too well to be laid aside. If Henry had been a strong leader with aggressive policies, his opposition could not have mustered the power it had by the late 1450s. But Henry was clearly ineffectual against his political opponents. His efforts at compromise were often ludicrous, and none was as widely derided as his declaration of Love Day on March 25, 1458.

Love Day was an optimistic medieval custom designed to heal wounds and effect reconciliation. On March 25, Henry invited the rival factions to walk arm in arm to St. Paul's Cathedral. A grand procession was led by the opulently robed king, wearing his crown, followed by the queen on the arm of Richard, duke of York. Behind them trailed a long parade of mutual enemies, hand in hand. One poet spoke for the king's naïve hope:

> At Poules in London, with gret renoun,
>> On oure ladi day in lente this peas was wrought;
> The Kynge, the Quene, with lordes many oone,
>> To worship that virgine as thei ought,
>> Wenten a procession, and sporiden right nought,
>>> In sighte of all the Comynalte,
>> In token that love was in herte and thought.
>>> Rejoise, Anglond, in concord & unite.

Another poet more accurately perceived no concord and unity in England, only

> ffayned frenship & ypocrisye;
> Also gyle on every side,
> With murdre & much pride;
>
> Great envy & wilfulnes,
> With-out mercy or rightwysnes;
> The cause is for lak of light . . .[14]

IV

Troublous Times

THE "LAK OF LIGHT" that darkened England in the late 1450s
worried and frightened Margaret Beaufort. Despite the protec-
tection of her brother-in-law, Jasper Tudor, and despite the thick
walls of Pembroke, she knew that another marriage would best secure
the future for herself and her son. Her large inheritances made her
less interested in accruing wealth than in aligning herself with a family whose influence and power would not be threatened by the Yorkists. Margaret chose, finally, to marry Sir Henry Stafford, whose
family carried on the title of duke of Buckingham.

From the mid fourteenth century, the Staffords had been noted
statesmen and soldiers in the service of a succession of kings. They
had married with other wealthy and important families, and their
inherited land and incomes made it possible for Humphrey Stafford,
the first duke of Buckingham, to be among the richest and most
powerful landlords when he came into his mother's legacy in 1438.
Unlike many of the nobility, Stafford did not choose to take sides
when the Wars of the Roses began in 1455. Though he never shrank
from war and was remembered for particular virulence in the fight
against Joan of Arc in the late 1420s, he determined that it was probably wise and in his best interests to remain outside the conflict. Still,
he was a confidant of Henry VI and was never far from the important court happenings. He was occupied, too, with his own family
and the marriages of his many children. His eldest son, Humphrey,
married a cousin of Margaret Beaufort's, the daughter of Edmund
Beaufort, duke of Somerset. His third son, Sir Henry Stafford, in
1459 ended Margaret's widowhood of just three years.

Sir Henry appears to have been a mild man with little involvement in public affairs. Unlike his brother Humphrey, he seems not to have taken an active role in the Wars, but spent much time with his wife at their various estates, some of which were given to the couple as a marriage gift by Sir Henry's father. Though she fulfilled her duties as a nobleman's wife — supervising the household, substituting for her husband in running the estates, raising her child — those tasks were only part of Margaret's life. In the early years of their marriage, Margaret resumed some of the scholarly work that had occupied her youth. She began translating one book of *The Imitation of Christ* which had been rendered into French and concerned herself with devising "practical schemes for the welfare of the surrounding labourers and her dependents." [1]

Both scholarly translations and medieval "social work" were pursuits more often associated with men, and more specifically with clergymen, than with women. Those intellectual endeavors, however, Margaret carried out alone. While her husband may have been encouraging, there is no evidence that their marriage was a union of like spirits resulting in a remarkable companionship. Margaret was as solitary in her marriage as she had been throughout her youth, and continued to live according to her own precepts.

She was determined to impart those precepts to her son. The wardship of Henry Tudor was never awarded by the king to a deserving nobleman. The child was, in effect, under the protection of his uncle, Jasper Tudor, who would have been a likely choice as guardian. Henry VI's decision to leave the boy with his mother shaped the child's character in a way far different from what it might otherwise have been. One of the acknowledged purposes of a boy's wardship was to provide an opportunity for him to learn the arts of war by being in the home of a noble commander and veteran. As earl of Pembroke, Jasper Tudor amply filled that role:

> The Erle of Pembroke curtys and firce;
> A-cross the mast he hyeth travers,
> The good shyp for to lede.

But his influence was tempered by the presence of Margaret herself, with whom Henry lived at least part of each year. Her son never forgot her gentle teachings, her high moral standards, and her exemplary intellectual life.

* * *

Margaret had already seen a husband and an uncle felled by the growing conflict between the Lancastrians and the Yorkists. In the summer of 1460, the war struck her life again.

On July 10 the armies clashed at Northampton. The king was accompanied by notable lords, among them Henry Stafford's father, Humphrey, duke of Buckingham, who had at last decided to inter vene in the Wars on behalf of the Lancastrians. The fighting lasted no more than half an hour, and the king's retinue was destroyed. Margaret's father-in-law was slain. Henry VI himself was taken prisoner. The defeat was a severe blow to the Lancastrian cause and the first major Yorkist victory. A Yorkist poet celebrated:

> Where-of god of his speciall grace,
>   Heryng the peple crying for mercye,
> Considering the falsehode in every place,
>   Gave infleweinz of myrthe into bodyes on hye.
>   The which in a berward * lighted prevelye,
> Edward,† yong of age, disposed in solace,
>   In hauking & hunting to begynne meryly,
>   To Northampton with the bere‡ he toke his trace . . .
> . . . The bere made the dogges to cry,
>   And with his pawme cast theyme to grounde.
>   The game was done in a litel stounde,
>   The buk** was slayne, & borne away . . .[2]

During a tense summer, the Yorkists ruled in the name of Richard. Their duke was then in Ireland, where he had fled in 1459 when Henry VI, convinced by his queen and his own supporters, finally had passed a bill of attainder against him. Traitors could not be delivered to the king from Ireland, where York was further protected by powerful friends and allies. By September, York had assembled considerable support. From a Kentish port, to which he had sailed from Ireland, he rode with an entourage of about five hundred to London. Preceded by trumpeters and mounted soldiers trailing banners, York came at last to claim the crown.

He marched to Westminster Palace, approached the empty throne,

---

* berward: Edward, who had joined with Warwick, the bear.

† Edward, then eighteen, York's eldest son, afterward Edward IV.

‡ The bear is associated with Richard Neville, earl of Warwick, whose arms carry a bear chained to a gnarled trunk.

** Henry, duke of Buckingham.

and laid his hand upon it for the first time. To all who stood gaping at his boldness, he announced that he had the right, by inheritance, to the crown of England. He claimed that Henry VI's grandfather, when he usurped the throne from Richard II, had done so at the expense of the Mortimers, Richard II's rightful heirs. Henry V had had no more claim to the throne than had his father, and Henry VI likewise illegally ruled the land. Richard of York compared England to a mortally ill patient, for whom he was physician.

> I declare and publish to you, that here I sit, as in the place
> to me by very justice lawfully belongyng, & here I rest, as he
> to whome this chayre of right apperteineth, not as he, which
> requireth of you favor, parcialitie, or bearynge, but egall
> right, frendly indifferencie, and trew administracion of jus-
> tice: for I beyng the partye greved and complaynaunt, can
> not minister to my self the Medecine . . . Nor yet this noble
> realme, and our naturall countrey shall never be unbukeled
> from her quotidian fever, except I (as the principall Physician
> & you, as trew and trusty Appotecaries) consult together, in
> makyng of the pocion, and trye out the clene and pure stuffe,
> from the old, corrupt, and putrified dregges. For undoubtedly,
> the rote & botome of this long festured cankar, is not yet
> extirpat . . . which hath bene and is the daily destruccion of
> the nobilitie, and the quotidian confusion of ye pore com-
> munaltie of this realme and kyngdom . . .[3]

A strange occurrence, coincident with York's lengthy oration, was taken as an omen of events to come. At a meeting of the commons, a crown set high above the assembly, which was used for holding tapers, suddenly fell down "without touche of any creature, or rigor of wynd." At that very moment, it was reported, a crown that adorned the Castle of Dover also suddenly, and with no apparent cause, crashed to the earth. Those who heard of the odd happenings speculated that "the Croune of the Realme should bee divided and changed, from one line to another."[4]

Those who witnessed York's speech were shocked and dumbstruck, "as though their mouths had been sowed up." They could not dethrone a living king, the ruler to whom they had sworn unalterable allegiance. They proposed, instead, that Richard allow Henry to wear the crown until his natural death. Then, Richard himself and his heirs would inherit the kingdom. York agreed to the compromise. Henry VI also agreed, thus refusing the throne for his small son.

The Wars of the Roses would have ended then, in the fall of 1460, were it not for Margaret of Anjou. She could not bear the idea that the crown would be denied her son. During the king's imprisonment she had fled at great peril with young Edward toward Wales, where she knew that Jasper Tudor and his men would protect them. She sought refuge at Harlech Castle, the seemingly impenetrable castle that once had been the main base of the legendary Welsh leader Owen Glendower, and there devised a strategy to retain the crown for her son.

Many of Margaret Beaufort's family rallied behind Margaret of Anjou, ready to fight in her name and in the name of the king. In part, they felt a real loyalty to Henry VI; in part, they were fighting for Margaret Beaufort and for her son. If Henry VI and the young prince Edward were killed, Margaret Beaufort would be compelled to come forth and claim the Lancastrian crown. It was clear to all who knew her that she would pass the crown to her son rather than rule in her own name. With Henry Tudor hardly more than a toddler, the Lancastrians could hope for little support among the nobility if he were presented as king. Even Margaret Beaufort herself, despite her aversion to the ruthless strategy plotted by Margaret of Anjou, hoped that the queen's troops would be victorious.

By the end of December, York had retired to his castle in Yorkshire. There he was challenged by the queen's army at Wakefield. Though many of his men were dispersed to attend to local skirmishes, which were increasingly prevalent in that time of upheaval, York decided to take up the challenge.

The Yorkists descended to a field between the castle and the town of Wakefield. Once in the open, they found themselves surrounded on all sides by Lancastrians. York felt "like a fish in a net, or a deere in a buckestall," [5] yet fought bravely. Within half an hour, the duke himself was slain and his army defeated. York was decapitated, his head crowned with a rude paper coronet, placed on a pole, and presented to the victorious queen. Then it was impaled on one of the gates of the city of York, through which Margaret's troops triumphantly marched south, pillaging and plundering as they went.

Mercenary armies on both sides were feared and hated by the commoners. These soldiers were recruited from the bottom of society, and however noble their leaders might have been, their troops could not be held back from robbery and rape. Margaret's men were among the worst. "The pepill in the northe robbe and styll, and ben apoynted to pill all thys cwntre, and gyffe a way menys goods and lufflords in all the sowth cwntre more than iiij or v. shers, for they wold be up on the men in northe, for it ys for the welle of all the sowthe." [6]

The two armies were soon to clash again. York's cause was taken up by Edward, his nineteen-year-old son, who led the Yorkist army against Jasper Tudor and his Welsh and Irish supporters on February 2, 1461. The battle began at ten in the morning in a field near Mortimer's Cross and ended in Tudor's defeat. The Yorkist victory was important for Edward, but even more important was a curious celestial sight. The sun suddenly appeared to him as three suns, and then just as suddenly joined as one. Edward was profoundly impressed and took the vision to be an omen of good fortune. Thereafter he included the sun in his badge.

Jasper Tudor's participation in the Wars was trying for his former sister-in-law, Margaret. In many ways, she depended on him more than she did on her husband, Henry Stafford. Jasper was closer to the intrigues of Henry VI's court, a valued aide of Margaret of Anjou, and a powerful commander. Without him, Margaret Beaufort would have felt more vulnerable than she did to attack by the Yorkists. Without his advice and reassurance, she would not have been able intelligently to assess real danger.

With great relief, she learned that he was not slain at Mortimer's Cross. Another Tudor, however, did not fare as well. Foremost among the Lancastrians fighting at that battle was Owen Tudor, long exiled in Wales, stepfather of Henry VI and Margaret Beaufort's one-time father-in-law. Tudor was captured, taken to Hereford, and condemned to death. It is alleged that as he laid his head on the block, he said that it was "wont to lie in queen Catherine's lap." When his head was displayed on the highest step of the market cross at Haverfordwest, a woman came each day to comb the hair, wash the face, and place around it a circle of lighted candles. Even in death Owen Tudor lost none of his charm.

The battle of Mortimer's Cross fired the Yorkists' cause, but two weeks later, at St. Albans, the site of the first York-Lancaster confrontation, their army was routed by a surprise attack. Henry was liberated by his queen, and Margaret's troops withdrew north to reassemble and make new plans.

The battle, which appears to have been no more than a skirmish in the St. Albans marketplace, did not dull Edward's sense of victory. The Yorkists were gaining considerable support where it mattered most — in the cities. Edward's triumph in early February gave him sufficient cause for celebration to allow him to ride into London and be warmly welcomed and hailed not only as victor, but as king. "He was so much esteemed, bothe of the nobilitie and commonaltie, for his liberalitie, clemencie, integrite, and corage, that above all other, he was extolled and praysed to the very heaven." [7] Men pledged more than their loyalty; they willingly wagered their lives and livelihood on his cause. Edward was a virile and vital figure, the most handsome prince that the French historian Comines, for one, had ever seen. "The lusty King Edward," Hall dubbed him, and his presence was an exciting change from the enervated Henry VI.

Clearly, London was rallying behind the young Yorkist rather than maintaining allegiance to the Lancastrian king. Londoners would gladly exchange the forty-year-old monarch, enfeebled by bouts of madness, dominated by a shrew and her raucous army, for a youth "of visage lovely, of body mighty, strong, and clean made." [8] They were inspired by Edward just as their grandfathers had been inspired by the young Henry V.

Edward, carrying on his father's dream, based his claim to the crown on heredity. For many Englishmen, however, heredity played a smaller role in pledging allegiance than did political expediency. Edward knew that with support in the capital, he was assured of being accepted as monarch throughout the land. On March 4, 1461, the young York heir had himself proclaimed king.

Lord Fauconbridge, addressing a large assembly in St. John's field, whipped the crowd into an emotional rejection of Henry VI. He "demaunded of the people, whether they woulde have the sayd kyng Henry to rule and reigne any lenger over them: To whom they with a whole voyce, aunswered, nay, nay." Then he asked if they were prepared to "serve, love, and obey" Edward. In a great outburst, they cried, "Yea, Yea, King Edward," shouting and applauding and tossing their caps into the air. After the acclaim, Edward and his supporters informed the nobility of the assent of the commons, and at Baynard's Castle Edward spoke to his peers.

An instinctive politician, Edward, after a long, pregnant pause, first thanked God for help in bringing him to victory. Then he acknowledged with deep gratitude the help of the multitude standing before him. He demurely wondered whether his shoulders were broad enough to bear such a burden and whether he would be able to lead them effectively, but the noblemen would hear no self-doubt. Pressed to accept their acclaim, Edward in the end agreed to taken on himself the weighty responsibility of the crown of England.

The next day "with great solempnitie, he was conveyed to Westmynster, and there set in the hawle, with the scepter royall in his hand, where, to all the poeple which there in great number were assembled, his title and clayme to the croune of England, was declared by ii. maner of wayes: the first, as sonne and heyre to duke Richard his father, right enheritor to thesame: the second, by aucthoritie of Parliament and forfeiture committed by, kyng Henry." [9]

Quickly the new king dispatched his troops northward to make a final conquest of the Lancastrians. The clash was thunderous. At Towton, on Palm Sunday, March 29, 1461, the greatest battle of the Wars was fought.

Though chronicles of diverse political persuasions put the number of soldiers involved as high as two hundred thousand, most probably fifty or sixty thousand men were involved in battle; many of these, especially on the Lancastrian side, were archers. There was a blinding snowstorm as the men approached each other, with wind blowing snow toward the advancing Lancastrians. The archers could hardly see their enemy, and their arrows never reached the intended victims. Instead, the snow allowed the Yorkists to approach more closely than they otherwise might have dared, and when the archers had spent their arrows, the Yorkists poured in to demolish them. Ten hours later, tens of thousands lay dead, their bodies bloodying the new-fallen snow.

> The northern party made them strong with spere & with sheld;
> On palmesonday affter the none thei met us in the feld.
> With-in an owre thei were right fayne to fle & ike to yeld —
> xxvii thousand the rose kyld in the feld.[10]

Edward's show of strength had so impressed some Lancastrian supporters that many changed their allegiance after Towton. Henry VI, Margaret of Anjou, their son, and several noblemen fled into Scotland. Edward IV returned to London.

The rose came to love london, ful ryally rydyng.
ii erchbisshops of england thei crowned the rose kyng.[11]

On June 28, 1461, London witnessed the formal coronation of the first Yorkist king.

V

While Lions War

FTER MORTIMER'S CROSS and his father's execution, Jasper
Tudor realized that he was in imminent danger of being arrested and executed. Fearing for his young nephew, Henry Tudor, as well as for himself, he easily convinced Margaret Beaufort of the need for greater protection for her son than could be offered at Pembroke. He insisted that she allowed him to take the boy with him to Harlech, where Margaret of Anjou had taken refuge with her son the year before.

In 1461 the castle was under the protection of Dafydd ab Einon, whose valor was widely praised. It was said of him that he once held a castle in France so long that all the old women of Wales gossiped about it. At Harlech, he claimed that he would hold it until all the old women of France would know of his courage. But Dafydd ab Einon was finally defeated in battle by a fellow Welshman and former Lancastrian, William Herbert.

Herbert had fought beside Edward IV at Mortimer's Cross and soon afterward was appointed Edward's counselor and chief justice in South Wales. He became the first Welshman to join the English peerage when, in 1461, Edward created him a baron. His wealth increased proportionately to his elevated title. From being merely a rich landowner he became, by 1468, the wealthiest magnate in Wales, with an annual income of £2400. Though he had once been a friend of Edmund Tudor's, Herbert's new identity made him an avowed enemy of all Lancastrians.

In September 1461, Herbert, called Black William because of his thick black hair and beard, gained a firmer footing in government when he was awarded, as remuneration for his invaluable service to the king, the castle and town of Pembroke, almost deserted after the flight of Jasper Tudor. More significantly, in February 1462 he obtained the wardship of Henry Tudor.

The young boy, just past his fifth birthday, was taken from his uncle's side and returned to his birthplace. Stripped of his title of earl of Richmond, which he had inherited from his father, at Pembroke he was both ward and prisoner.

It is doubtful that Henry's mother was allowed to live at Pembroke. Margaret Beaufort would have readily given up her own liberty to join her son, but it is more likely that she and Henry Stafford withdrew to one of their own estates, where they would be less visible and less vulnerable. Jasper Tudor had convinced her that as long as Edward IV believed he enjoyed widespread support, he had no need to consider the young Henry Tudor a threat.

The pain of separation from her child was partially assuaged for Margaret by Jasper's total devotion to his nephew. He promised her that if there was any danger to Henry, he would not hesitate to remove him, forcibly if necessary, from Pembroke. In reality, safekeeping in the home of a prominent Yorkist was not a misfortune for the young Beaufort heir. The Herberts, Jasper assured Margaret, were growing closer to the king. There were even rumors, as time went on, that Herbert meant Henry to be the husband of his daughter Maud.

Though Henry was essentially a captive, his life under the Herberts was not harsh. Herbert's wife, Anne, grew genuinely fond of her young charge and engaged able tutors for him. He had the companionship of the Herbert children and the security of the attendance of his own nurse.

Edward IV saw his Welsh ally as an important adviser — as trusted as his cousin, the powerful magnate Richard Neville, earl of Warwick, whose success at aiding the Yorkists earned him the nickname the King-Maker. "The said Earle of Warwicke might justly be called King Edward's father," wrote Comines, "as also for the great services he did him, for the which the King had also highly advaunced him." [1] The friendship between the king and Herbert, a man Warwick saw as an upstart and opportunist, angered Warwick. It was not long before he and Herbert became rivals. One point of contention was the prospective marriage of the king.

The marriage was seen as a possible means for solidifying relations with potential allies. Warwick believed that a match must be made with a princess of France and began to negotiate for a marriage between Edward and Bona of Savoy, the sister of Louis XI, a monarch so distrusted that he was dubbed "the universal spider." In his late thirties when he ascended the French throne, Louis had been an outspoken adversary of his father, Charles VII, repeatedly intriguing against him. He could be gregarious and voluble among his peers, but in matters of diplomacy and international relations he was secretive and deceitful. Warwick hoped for an alliance with France and her crafty king.

Herbert, on the other hand, believed that an alliance should be effected between England and the large, sprawling territory of Burgundy, encompassing two great blocs in eastern France and the Low Countries, including Flanders, Holland, and Brabant. The English economy was highly dependent on trade with Flemish ports and, Herbert reasoned, would do well to nurture good relations with the Burgundian leader, Duke Philip the Good.

Because France and Burgundy were the bitterest of enemies, it was not possible for England to claim alliance with both. And because Warwick and Herbert maintained such strong preferences in the selection of a royal bride, it was certain that they, too, would become enemies.

Edward, while he humored the recommendations of his cousin and his friend, continued to court some of the more attractive noblewomen who surrounded him, and earned a reputation for "fleshlie wantonnesse." He was attractive to women not only because of his power and might, but his youth, manliness, and apparently handsome looks. For all his dalliance, however, neither Warwick nor Herbert would have guessed that he would marry for any reason other than the good of England.

* * *

In 1464, while Edward was hunting in the forest of Whittlebury, he saw an attractive young woman waiting beneath the spread of a magnificent oak. She had come, she told him, to plead with the king "that she might be restored unto such small lands as her late husband had given her in jointure." [2] Her husband, Edward soon learned, had been Sir John Grey, a Lancastrian who had been killed at the second battle of St. Albans. She herself had been a lady in waiting to Queen Margaret. Now a dowager, Elizabeth Woodville had come to the king as a last resort to regain her legacy.

Edward was sympathetic to her cause and undeniably attracted to the young widow. She was stylishly dressed in a long, flowing, high-waisted gown. Her hairline had been painstakingly plucked to reveal a broad white brow beneath an ornate headdress. Five years older than the king, at twenty-seven Elizabeth had a gentle beauty and winning manner. "She was a woman more of formal countenaunce than of excellent beautie," the chronicler Edward Hall recorded, "and yet of such beautie & favor, that, with her sober demeanure, lovely lokyng, and femynyne smylyng, (neither to wanton nor to humble) besyde her toungue so eloquent, and her wit so pregnant, she was able to ravishe the mynde of a meane person, when she allured and made subject to her, the hart of so great a king." Edward "considered all the linyamentes of her body, and the wise and womanly demeanure that he saw in her" [3] and decided she would be his mistress.

Elizabeth claimed to be overwhelmed by the king's attentions but, unlike so many other women, would not give herself to him illicitly. She said that she thought herself "too simple to be his wife [but] too good to be his concubine." [4] She allowed him to continue seeing her, often meeting under the tree that became the legendary "queen's oak," and kept the flirtation chaste. For Edward, a virtuous woman was even more attractive than the accessible gentlewomen of the court, and he was overcome with love. In May 1464 he married her. On September 28, he announced the secret marriage to a shocked council.

Even Edward's mother, Cecily, duchess of York, was incensed at her son's foolish infatuation. She wanted him to make a politically astute match and, moreover, wanted him to marry a virgin. Since Elizabeth already had two children, and since Edward had already fathered two illegitimate children, Edward knew this union would not be barren — far more important to a monarch than his wife's purity.

Most angered of all the king's subjects was Warwick, at that moment in France, where his marriage proposition between Edward and Bona was "well liked . . . so that the matrimonie on that side was cleerlie assented to . . ." The news that Edward already had a wife arrived in a letter from trusted friends. Warwick now felt himself a fool. Relations with the French had been so shaky that they would no doubt believe there was some other motive for his being sent: ". . . it might be judged he came rather . . . to moove a thing never minded, and to treat a marriage determined before not to take effect." No one would believe that he, kinsman and counselor to the king, did not know of the king's intentions to wed a commoner. "He thought himselfe evill used, that when he had brought the matter to his purposed intent and wished conclusion, then to have it quaile on his part; so as all men might thinke at the least wise, that his prince made small account of him, to send him on such a sleevelesse errand." [5]

Warwick returned to England angry and distrustful, but still willing to claim himself a Yorkist. Edward IV's reign was precarious, and Warwick's presence among his allies was critical. His defection would have been a severe blow to the Yorkists, who had barely managed to crush rebellion after rebellion incited by Lancastrians throughout the countryside. Warwick was a natural leader. Though he was extremely wealthy, his generosity and fairness exempted him from the hatred and envy that had been accorded such men as the ill-fated Suffolk. The common people thought Warwick could never fail, "and that without hym, nothing to be well done. For which causes his aucthoritie shortly so fast increased that whiche waie he bowed, that waye ranne the streame, and what part he avaunced, that side got the superioritie." [6]

Despite his awareness of Warwick's value to him, Edward allowed others to benefit more from his attentions. Repeatedly Warwick felt that he was being overlooked in favor of the ubiquitous Woodvilles. Elizabeth's sisters, brothers, uncles were all elevated beyond their original rank, provoking much jealousy among the old nobility. Even more disturbing to Warwick was Edward's arrangement of a marriage between his sister Margaret and Charles, earl of Charolais, the son of the duke of Burgundy, and the intended match between Charolais's daughter and Edward's youngest brother, George, duke of Clarence. Warwick had planned that Clarence would marry his own Anne, and feared that his daughter would have a poor chance of making a good match, with all the high-ranking young men being given to Woodville women.

While Edward delayed in marrying his brother to the Burgundian heiress, Warwick closed in and bound Clarence to Anne. Once she and Clarence were married, the young man was persuaded to join Warwick in his calculations against the king.

Louis XI had made attractive offers to Warwick, promising extensive aid if he would lead an insurrection against the king and replace on the throne the pro-French and more malleable Henry VI. Warwick's reward would be two huge principalities and the solid alliance with France. On July 20, 1469, with the hope of glory and grandeur, Warwick marched in defiance to London.

Rumors of Warwick's defection alarmed Margaret Beaufort. Although she prayed for the restoration of Henry VI, she feared for her son if Edward felt himself threatened. William Herbert himself would be fighting in the king's name. Unless Warwick defeated the Yorkist in a bold, first strike, Henry VI's cause — and Margaret's own — would be lost. No one knew how strong Warwick was, though speculations abounded.

Herbert, reinforced by the earl of Devon, awaited his encounter with Warwick at Banbury. Unfortunately Devon had quarreled with Herbert the evening before battle over a barmaid at the local inn; Devon had left, taking his reinforcements with him. Herbert, severely hampered, was easily defeated by Warwick's troops. With Herbert's beheading, Warwick succeeded in ridding England of his strongest enemy — save Edward IV himself.

Having believed that Herbert's defense could not fail, Edward did not surround himself with troops and arms. When Warwick confronted him, he did not resist, knowing that armed combat would do no good; what he needed, more than anything, was time. He was brought to Warwick Castle, then to Middleham, a virtual fortress, where he was to have been kept prisoner while Warwick ruled.

But popular sentiment, always unstable, had turned against the King-Maker. Local uprisings threatened to undermine Warwick's rebellion, and only the presence of the king could calm the people. Edward was allowed more freedom and was transferred to Pontefract Castle. There, he managed to gather a great many noblemen still loyal to his party. Though he made no overt move to quash the rebels, he ensured that they could go no further in their plans.

By the spring of 1470, Warwick realized that Edward had gained enough strength to doom his rebellion and began to consider more drastic measures to make certain his success. He fled to France, where Louis XI was more than willing to aid him — but only on the condition that he reconcile himself with a woman he hated: Margaret of Anjou.

Warwick was gone for some four months, during which Margaret Beaufort suffered great anxiety over the fate of her son. She did not know whether the arrogant Margaret of Anjou, used to wielding power in her own name, would agree to a partnership with Warwick.

The queen might well believe that she alone could restore her husband to the throne and safeguard that throne for her son. But Margaret Beaufort was also the mother of a potential heir to the crown of England, and she too shared a mother's ambitions for her son. She believed, though, that those ambitions could not be realized through ruthless killings and wanton violence. Warwick might temper the queen's wrath with political strategy. Together, they might save the Lancastrian throne. Alone, Margaret of Anjou would doubtless fail.

Louis XI prepared the exiled English queen for the meeting with her great enemy. With ambition before pride, Warwick agreed to do anything necessary to defeat Edward IV, even to kneel before the haughty Margaret of Anjou and beg forgiveness. His submission swayed the queen. In a cautious and cool encounter, Margaret and Warwick swore allegiance to one another and to England, praying before an alleged relic of the true cross that God might give them the strength and good fortune to bring Henry VI again to the throne.

In September, Warwick sailed for England, finding Edward IV unprepared for this invasion. He had little trouble entering London, marching northward, and defeating the few troops that were surprised to encounter him. Edward could do nothing but flee. He left for exile in France with two ships and some seven hundred supporters, taking nothing but what they had worn in battle. They had little money and only one hope: a welcome at their destination, the court of Edward's sister Margaret in Burgundy.

Edward's most faithful supporter at that moment was his brother Richard of Gloucester, who stood beside him as he stepped off the ship and onto Burgundian soil. Neither could pay the captain, but the king gave him a gown trimmed with martin and the promise of one day aiding him in turn. The refugees were warmly received. Charles the Bold, the powerful duke of Burgundy, eager to stop Warwick and Henry VI in their alliance with France, promised to supply his English daughter-in-law's brother with men and arms.

With Edward out of the country, Warwick gained new power. He marched to the Tower of London and freed the former king. Henry, more bewildered than angry, was persuaded to dress in a long gown of blue velvet, take to his horse, and ride through the streets of London to St. Paul's. He drew an exuberant, if incredulous, crowd, who immediately took up the cry "God save King Harry!"

Now that Henry VI was restored to the throne, Warwick was given high responsibility in government. The ousted Lancastrians once more came into their titles and property and could once again live in freedom. Jasper Tudor and Henry Tudor were re-created earls, and Pembroke Castle was returned to them. A joyful Margaret Beaufort was reunited with her fourteen-year-old son after nearly nine years' separation.

Henry Tudor was very much his mother's child: quiet, introspective, with an inner strength nurtured by years of emotional solitude. He was well aware of the political maelstrom of which he might easily become the center, but he lacked the swagger and arrogance that many said characterized the Lancastrian prince Edward, also more his mother's child than his father's. Henry had a calm yet competent presence, an integrity about which his mother was relieved and proud.

She knew, however, that although Henry VI reigned, his rival was still alive and gathering strength in Burgundy. Henry Tudor's position was no more secure now than it had been throughout the reign of Edward IV. Should battle begin again, his position would be considerably more dangerous. She did not reveal her fears to her son but was quick to divulge them to her brother-in-law.

Jasper, of course, was aware of his nephew's precarious situation. Even Henry VI, though he knew that his crown should pass to his own son, doubted that Prince Edward would survive to become king. When, for the first time, Jasper Tudor brought his nephew to court to meet the reinstated monarch, the king is said to have placed his hands on the youth's head, softly prophesying:

> Make much of him, my lords; for this is he
> Must help you more than you are hurt by me.[7]

Henry's second reign was destined to be brief. For months he had urged his exiled queen, still in France, to sail with their son to England. Finally, with much apprehension, Margaret of Anjou agreed, but a storm turned her back, delaying her arrival until April 13, 1471. Even as she sailed, another fleet of ships was bringing her husband's enemies, some twelve hundred strong, to the same shores. Edward, aided by the Burgundians and his allies at home, was prepared to meet Warwick with force. On Easter Sunday, April 14, the two armies clashed at Barnet.

In dense morning fog, Warwick assembled his men and urged that "they fight not onely for the libertie of the countreye agaynste a tiraunte, which wrongfullye and againste all right had invaded and subdued thys realme, but they fyght in the querel of a true and undubitate king against a cruell man and a torcious usurper; in the cause of a Godly and a pitiful Prince against an abominable man-queller and a bloudy boutcher . . ." [8] In ten years, Warwick had come full circle in his allegiance, but as he spoke, his men did not doubt that his loyalty was as deeply ingrained as if he had been born a Lancas-trian and had never strayed.

The battle began early and lasted well into the afternoon. Esti-mates of the number slain vary from one thousand to ten times that. Among the dead lay Richard Neville, the King-Maker himself.

The Lancastrians still would not concede defeat. Their young prince, the eighteen-year-old son of Henry VI and Margaret of An-jou, prevailed on his mother to call forth more troops and continue fighting. From Barnet, some twenty miles north of London, the Lan-castrians were faced with a decision in strategy. They knew they could not proceed south, where the Yorkists had gained their greatest popularity in the capital, but must attempt, instead, to join the Welsh Lancastrians — Jasper Tudor and his followers — near the border. To go north, however, meant crossing the Severn, no easy matter since many of the crossing towns were strongly Yorkist. Never-theless, the troops headed north, and Edward IV, guessing correctly their move, followed them. By May 3, the two sides were advancing in parallel lines, the Yorkists high on a Cotswold slope, the Lancastri-ans in the Severn vale. The spring day was unseasonably hot, and both armies were exhausted as they made their way upstream along the Severn. They could not drink the waters, which their own horses had fouled. They could not rest.

By evening, the Lancastrians had arrived at Tewkesbury but were too spent to attempt a crossing. The Yorkists had overtaken them. There was no choice but to prepare for battle. Early the next day Edward began to advance on his enemy. The Lancastrians were as-sembled on a low ridge with the town at their backs. Edward assigned some two hundred cavalry to remain hidden in Tewkesbury Park. His other troops opened with a round of cannon fire and arrows.

From her perch on the roof of a nearby house, the Lancastrian queen watched as her men were slain in vicious hand-to-hand com-bat. Margaret of Anjou saw her only son taken prisoner and then, in despair, fled to a nearby nunnery, Little Malvern Priory, for refuge. She knew then that her cause was irreversibly defeated.

The young Edward was brought before Edward IV. How, asked the king, did he dare to return to England and defy the crown? Margaret's son replied, as Henry IV had once retorted, that he had come only to claim his father's inheritance — but his meaning was clear. The king was outraged; he struck the youth across the face with his gauntlet and condemned him to death. Margaret was found in the priory and taken with the triumphant troops to London.

By May 21, Edward IV, having assembled his entourage, rode in victory to the capital. The next evening Henry VI, at prayer in the Tower, was surprised by an armed henchman and fatally stabbed. The meek, mild man who should never have been king was finally dead. His heir was dead, and for many in England the Lancastrian claim to the throne was dead. Shakespeare allowed Henry to speak his own epitaph:

> O piteous spectacle! O bloody times!
> While lions war and battle for their dens,
> Poor harmless lambs abide their enmity.
> Weep, wretched man, I'll aid thee tear for tear;
> And let our hearts and eyes, like civil war,
> Be blind with tears, and break o'ercharg'd with grief . . .
>
> Sad-hearted men, much overgone with care,
> Here sits a king more woeful than you are.[9]

VI

The Thorn

FOR HENRY TUDOR, the only Lancastrian rival to Yorkist Edward IV, even the often-ignored countryside of Wales was no longer safe enough. Jasper believed that his nephew must be removed, at whatever peril, to France. At first Margaret resisted; she had been separated from her son for too long. Never having been abroad, she feared for his safety outside England. But Jasper, wise to the machinations of the court, soon convinced his former sister-in-law that there was no alternative but flight.

The king, he told her, was becoming increasingly suspicious of dissension and quick to react to any threat of insurrection. He had been caught unaware by Warwick but had sworn not to repeat his mistake. Many expressed concern about the repressive atmosphere. In September 1471, John Paston warned his brother: "Ther is moche adoo in the Northe, as men seyn. I pray you be ware off your guydyng, and in chyff of yowre langage, so that from hense forthe by your langage noo men perceyve that ye favor any person contrary to the Kynges plesure." [1]

In late May 1471, Jasper Tudor retreated to Pembroke and assembled local supporters, an unruly mob armed with pitchforks and billhooks, to defend himself and Henry during their short journey to the coast. Margaret accompanied them to the port of Tenby, where, on June 2, she said farewell to her cherished fifteen-year-old son, whom she feared she might never see again.

Since Edward had strongly allied himself with Burgundy, the Tudors believed they would be favorably received by France and made that country their destination. But an improvident storm prevented their landing at a French port and shifted their course toward Brittany. Here, they were less sure of their reception.

Duke Francis II of Brittany was an avowed enemy of France and therefore a friend of Burgundy and England. Louis XI made no secret of his desire to conquer Brittany, and the small duchy was in need of powerful allies. But Edward IV's claim to the English crown was not convincing to the wary Bretons. They did not dare to alienate his rival, because that rival might soon wear Edward's crown. When Jasper and Henry landed, they were treated hospitably, if not warmly, and had no fear that they would be turned over to their enemies.

Margaret, though assured of her son's temporary safety, was continuously anxious about his welfare. Throughout the summer, she lived only for reports of him, which were brought by Lancastrian supporters from Brittany, France, or Flanders. In October 1471, her loneliness was increased by the death of her husband, Sir Henry Stafford. Now, without her son, her husband, her brother-in-law, she retired to her estates, far from the turbulence of Edward IV's London. Her life revolved around only two interests: her son and religion.

Prayer, always central to Margaret Beaufort's life, now took on new importance. She began rising earlier to pray longer and began to spend more time at her evening devotions. She kept fasts strictly, went to confession frequently, and sometimes committed herself to the penance of wearing hair shirts. For a while, she resided at Torrington, where her land adjoined that of the local church. The clergyman impressed her with his need to live near his people in order to minister to them most effectively. Margaret donated her manor to the church, then moved on.

Aged thirty, she had seen enough to believe that no one could be trusted, that no reign was stable, that even brothers could turn against one another, that joy could quickly become despair. Her father, her first husband, her uncle, two fathers-in-law were victims of political violence, and she vowed to herself that she would not see her son fall victim to the same.

She sought solace in religion, sharing the sentiments of many poets of the age who sought to transcend the cruelty of the contemporary world through devotion to the higher values imparted in Christian teachings.

Truste ye rather to letters writen in th'is
Than to this wretched world, that full of sinne is.

It is fals in his beheste and right desceivable;
It hath begiled manye men, it is so unstable.

It is rather to beleve the waveringe wind
Than the chaungeable world, that maketh men so blind.[2]

For her son, however, Margaret wanted to provide the safety and security that could come only with political stability, the end of the Wars and control, finally, of his own destiny. She would not allow him to be deceived by wealth, illusory power, or false friends. Loneliness and ignominy had threatened him throughout his short life, just as they had threatened her.

Wholsom in smelling be the soote floures,
Full delitable, outward, to the sight;
The thorn is sharp, curyd with fresh coloures;
All is nat gold that outward sheweth bright;
A stokfish boon in dirknesse yeveth a light,
Twen fair and foul, as God list dispoose,
A difference atwix day and night —
All stant on chaung like a midsomer roose.[3]

She wanted Henry to live in a world different from the one into which he had been born. In the very act of naming him, she had attempted to affect his destiny. In the years since then, she had seen another mother, with an obsession as strong as her own, try to hold on to a kingdom for her child. Margaret of Anjou had failed. Her supporters were not friends; her friends had not been loyal. Too many had been involved in the Lancastrian queen's grandiose schemes to rule England. Her violence had been broad and undirected, turning away those who should have been sought for aid.

In Margaret of Anjou's failure, Margaret Beaufort learned a valuable lesson in political strategy. She would act for her son in the same way she conducted every other part of her own life: intelligently, meticulously, cautiously. For two years she quietly worked out her plans. Then, in 1473, she took a third husband.

Sir Thomas Stanley was a widower with a large family. Because he was a third cousin to Margaret — as Henry Stafford had been — a papal dispensation was necessary before the couple could marry. Such dispensations were common in a society where nobility married nobility almost exclusively and where, for generation upon generation, all were related. Permission from the pope came fairly promptly and was, as usual, reciprocated by a generous donation to the Church.

Stanley was a clever statesman and a trusted ally of Edward IV. His incisive mind earned him the nickname "the wily fox." Margaret did not want alliance with a Lancastrian who shied away from political involvement. She knew that if her son was to be protected, if he was ever to be allowed to return to England, he must have the support of a family in high esteem with the king. Though her own political loyalty never wavered from the Lancastrians, she allied herself with a prominent Yorkist to benefit only one person: her son. As Stanley's wife, Margaret would also be thrust into court life, where she could learn of political events firsthand.

Edward IV had sufficiently embroiled himself in international problems to distract his attention from Henry Tudor. The king was renewing efforts for a treaty with Burgundy to ensure that country's alliance in his planned invasion of France. He managed to effect the invasion in 1474, but Louis XI quashed what might have been a renewal of the old war by offering a lucrative bribe. By the Treaty of Picquigny, signed in August 1475, Edward was awarded a grand sum and an annual lifelong pension in exchange for dropping his claims to the French throne. In January 1476, he returned to the French their defeated princess, Margaret of Anjou, who was ransomed for fifty thousand crowns and who, in exchange for a small pension from the French king, was forced to relinquish all rights to her family's lands. Gradually, the widowed queen sank into poverty and died, a broken woman, in 1482.

Along with his political machinations, Edward's personal life was sufficiently tumultuous to turn his attentions from Margaret Beaufort's son, sole heir to Lancaster claims to his crown. By 1475, Elizabeth had borne five children, three daughters and two sons, the eldest of whom, Edward, was named prince of Wales and raised as heir apparent. In 1479 another daughter was born; the following year, the last child, Bridget, was carried to the christening font by Margaret Beaufort. One foreign visitor was struck by the apparent domestic felicity of the royal household, but the bliss was superficial. Despite the proliferation of children, Edward's devotion to Elizabeth had long since waned, and he began once again to take a succession of companions. "He was licentious in the extreme," reported the Italian historian Mancini; "moreover it was said that he had been most insolent to numerous women after he had seduced them, for, as soon as he grew weary of dalliance, he gave up the ladies much against their will to the other courtiers." [4] His last liaison was with Jane Shore, the wife of a London goldsmith.

Edward often boasted "that he had three concubines: one the merriest, another the wiliest, the third the holiest harlot in the realm, as one whom no man could get out of church lightly to any place, but it were to his bed." [5] Elizabeth Lucy, by whom he had a child, and Eleanor Butler were holy and wily; but Jane was by all accounts the merriest and his favorite. She had dark blond hair, a full oval face, piercing gray eyes. Even St. Thomas More could not but admit that there was "nothing in her body that you would have changed." [6] She was a perfect mistress: "her Body inclining to fat, her Skin smooth and white, her Countenance always enliven'd with an Air of Mirth and Cheerfulness, and agreeable to the Condition of a Woman who wanted nothing, and had it in her Power to Command every thing." [7]

Jane was witty, could read and write and keep up a sprightly conversation. Often she helped to reconcile Edward with some men who were out of his favor, obtained pardons, sued for redress. She clearly enjoyed her station. Centuries later an admiring poet revived her spirit:

> In Heart and Mind I did rejoyce,
> That I had made so sweet a Choice;
> And therefore did my stage resign,
> To be King Edward's Concubine . . .
>
> From City then to Court I went,
> To reap the Pleasures of Content;
> And had the Joys that Love could bring,
> And knew the Secretes of a king . . .[8]

But even Jane Shore could not mitigate the growing enmity between the king and his wayward brother George, duke of Clarence. Clarence had returned to the family fold after his defection to Warwick, but Edward IV knew that he could not be fully trusted. After his wife, Isabel, died, Clarence became more and more erratic and went so far as to execute one of his servants for allegedly poisoning his duchess. His paranoia became more general when he was rebuked in his efforts to arrange a second marriage with the daughter of the duke of Burgundy, whom Edward wanted to save for a Woodville. Clarence's hatred of the queen and her clan became increasingly annoying. Moreover, Edward was convinced that Clarence had aided some local rebellions against the throne. By 1478, Edward could no longer bear his brother's interference in his government; he attainted him, accused him of treason, and condemned him to death.

Much gossip surrounded the circumstances of Clarence's execution. A notorious drunkard, Clarence was said to have requested a butt of sweet wine, malmsey, into which he fell and drowned. (Historians now speculate that he may indeed have been drowned, but in his bath in prison.)

When it seemed that Edward's reign was at last secure, prospering, and relatively tranquil, the king's health began to decline markedly. Even his respected personal physician — one of three in attendance to the royal family at any time — could not help him. This "doctoure of physyque stondith muche in the presence of the kinges meles, by the councelying or answering to the kinges grace wich dyet is best according, and to the nature and operacion of all the metes. And comynly he shulk talke with the steward, chambrelayn, assewer, and the master cooke to devyse by counsayle what metes or drinkes is best according with the kinges dyet." [9] But a lifetime of dissolute living — Edward habitually used an emetic "for the delight of gorging his stomach once more" [10] — had taken its toll. Edward, greatly overweight and dissipated, succumbed to a sudden illness of debatable cause. Mancini claimed that Edward, already depressed by years of conflict with the French and Flemings, did not take proper care of himself when he went fishing one day on the river at Westminster. He "allowed the damp cold to strike his vitals . . . [and] there contracted the illness from which he never recovered, though it did not long afflict him." [11] Other observers thought he died from overindulgence of wine or even of vegetables. One sixteenth-century historian suspected poison.

The king had long realized the importance of providing for a stable rule if he should die during the minority of his eldest son, and in 1475 had composed a will that gave the greatest authority to his wife. But in later years he thought better of leaving the government in the hands of a woman so widely disliked. Codicils to his original testament place his trust in the brother who had stood beside him in peace and in war, a man he knew only as valiant, honest, and loyal: Richard, duke of Gloucester.

* * *

Edward's death on April 9, 1483, shocked the populace. Poets mourned the loss of their still-young king, who, though he had grown "corpulent and boorelie," nevertheless inspired their admiration.

> O noble Edward, wher art thowe be-come,
>> Which full worthy I have seen goyng in estate?
> Edward the iiiith I mene, with the sonne,
>> The rose, the sonne-beme, which was full fortunate.
>> Noon erthly prince durst make with hym debate.
>>> Art thowe agoo, and was here yestirday?
>>> All men of Englond ar bound for the to pray.
>
> The well of knyghthode, withouten any pere,
>> Of all erthely prynces thowe were the lode-sterre!
> Be-holde and rede, herkyn well and hyre!
>> In gestis, in romansis, in cronicles nygh and ferre,
>> Well knowen it is, there can no man it deferre,
>>> Perelees he was, and was here yestirday.
>>> All men of Englond ar bounde for hym to pray.
>
> ffy on this worlde! What may we wrecches say,
>> Thate nave have lost the lanterne and the light?
> Oure kyng oure lorde — alas, and wele-a-wey!
>> In every felde full redy for oure right;
>> It was no nede to pray hym for to fight;
>>> Redy he was, that was here yestirday.
>>> All men of Englond ar bounde for hym to pray.[12]

If the commoners mourned sincerely for their loss, the feelings of the nobility were mixed with concerns about their own state and station under a new realm. Elizabeth Woodville, well aware of the hatred she inspired among the old aristocracy, worried about her personal fate during the minority of her son. She had little faith in the man her husband had chosen as protector. Unlike Edward, she doubted Richard's real loyalty to the king's family. Nor was Elizabeth alone in her feelings toward Richard of Gloucester. Hardly any figure from the fifteenth century emerges shrouded in such mystery as the enigmatic brother of the dead king.

Though portraits of Richard show a well-formed, reasonably attractive young man, Richard, thirty-one when he assumed his protectorate, was described later as "little of stature, ill-featured of limbs, crook-backed, his left shoulder much higher than his right, hard favored of visage, and such as in states called warly . . . He was malicious, wrathful, envious, and from afore his birth ever proward." [13] He was said to have been born feet first, with teeth, to the great and unnatural pain of his mother. He was accused, later, of having actually committed the murder of his brother Clarence. But at the time he became guardian of the young prince of Wales, he was known only for his military competence and his courageous defense of the king's will.

If he stood loyally beside his brother until Edward's death, Richard's sentiments were completely reversed in April 1483. He did not want the protectorship of England; he wanted the crown. And he immediately summoned aid to effect his plans. He had to seek his aid from sources other than those powerful men who gathered around his nephew, fully believing the young boy to be the next king. Chief among those counselors were William Hastings, Bishop John Morton, and Sir Thomas Stanley, Margaret Beaufort's third husband.

Instead, Richard formed a close alliance with Henry Stafford, second duke of Buckingham, the nephew of Margaret Beaufort by her marriage to Sir Henry Stafford. For her part, Margaret's strongest ties were with supporters of the future Edward V. But she felt she understood her ambitious nephew better, perhaps, than he understood himself. She knew that his support of a Yorkist was not feigned, as was her own; but she doubted the depth of Buckingham's loyalty to the protector of England, believing his fealty to be based more on hatred for the Woodvilles than on love for England.

Buckingham, like Richard, detested the Woodvilles (although at the age of eleven he had been married to the queen's sister Katherine) because of Edward's patronage of the family. Of the thirty-five peerage titles created or revived during his short reign, Edward had bestowed most on his wife's family. Moreover, Edward had denied Buckingham accession to a grand inheritance, half of the de Bohun estates, to which he had been entitled since 1471, when Henry VI and his son were both slain. Apparently, Richard promised that those lands and revenues would be immediately turned over to the duke if he were king.

Two young boys stood in the way of Richard's accession to the throne. The twelve-year-old Prince Edward was at Ludlow, in Wales, under the tutelage of his uncle, the queen's brother Earl Rivers, when news came of his father's death and his imminent coronation. He prepared to journey to London, but the Woodvilles exercised extreme caution. It was not until late in the month that some two thousand soldiers had been assembled and proceeded to the capital.

On April 30, Earl Rivers, following his nephew's entourage, was intercepted by Richard with some three hundred soldiers and arrested. Richard and Buckingham then rode to Stony Stratford, where they overtook the prince, attended by Sir Thomas Vaughan, his chamberlain, and his half brother, Elizabeth's son by her first marriage, Sir Richard Grey.

Richard advised Prince Edward that a plot had been devised against him, in which both Vaughan and Grey were instrumental. Edward protested, but the atmosphere of doubt and suspicion was so thick that the youth was eventually convinced. Rivers and Grey were imprisoned at Pontefract, whose thick walls had already witnessed centuries of violence. On June 25, both were beheaded.

At first, Edward and his younger brother, Richard, were guarded at Stony Stratford. The queen and her other son, the marquis of Dorset, fled into sanctuary at Westminster, where frightening rumors reached them. In early May, when Richard and the duke of Buckingham finally arrived in London, the boy king had been moved to the Tower; his brother, to Westminster.

Because it was usual for a king to rest at the Tower before his coronation, Richard's removal there of his nephew was not seen as an act of rebellion. Edward was permitted to confer with his most trusted counselors: among them, Hastings, Morton, and Stanley. The coronation was set for late June, and the council debated over whether or not Richard's protectorate should continue for the entire minority of the king. Richard had no doubt the council would sanction his continuing as protector, but he grew increasingly suspicious that the intimate advisers surrounding the king were becoming overly sympathetic to the Woodvilles and would allow their influence in government to thwart his own eventual rule.

Those three advisers were closely watched. Each was influential; each, in his own way, could be a formidable opponent to Richard. Sir Thomas Stanley was wealthy, with large landholdings and great command over several key areas in England and Wales. He could assemble vast troops, if he were called on for aid, and could be indispensable in an insurrection. Bishop Morton combined the authority of the Church with a natural presence that inspired respect and deference. He had decided, as a boy, to devote himself to his country. "Having endured many changes of fortune," wrote his disciple

Thomas More, "he had acquired at great cost a vast stock of wisdom, which is not soon lost when purchased so dear." [14] He had been loyal to Henry VI, an active Lancastrian, but had been wooed by Edward IV to support the Yorkist cause when he became king. If Morton yielded because of expediency in 1461, he nevertheless had retained his own identity and inner strength.

In 1478, Morton's appointment as bishop of Ely had been celebrated with great pomp. The bishop walked barefoot the two miles from his palace at Downham to the cathedral and then, after the ceremonies, retired with his guests to the palace of Ely for a feast as grand as any that might be held at Westminster. Three courses, each comprising some dozen dishes, included venison, cygnet, pheasant, peacock, rabbit, perch, curlew, plover, crayfish, larks, and sturgeon. Though, as spokesman for the Church, he was concerned with extravagance and ostentation, decrying "the base avarice of a few," he admitted his weakness for fine fare, and his reputation as a gourmand was well known.

It was, in fact, the bishop's strawberries that Richard pretended to covet one June day when he interrupted a meeting of Hastings, Stanley, and Morton. "My lord," Gloucester said, "you have verie good strawberries at your garden in Holborn, I require you to let us have a mess of them." The request did not seem to surprise Morton, who replied, "Gladlie, my lord . . . would God I had some better thing as readie to your pleasure as that!" [15]

If Richard's craving did not upset Morton, it unnerved Stanley, who the night before had had an unsettling dream concerning himself and Hastings. He "thought that a boare with his tuskes so rased them both by the heads, that the bloud ran about both their shoulders. And forsomuch as the protector gave the boare for his cognisance, this dreame made so fearefull an impression in his heart, that he was throughlie determined no longer to tarie . . ." [16] He started from the dream before midnight, and immediately sent a messenger to Hastings, begging him to ride away with him. But Hastings refused. Now, as the men waited for Bishop Morton's servant to return with the strawberries and for Richard to come back to claim them, Stanley wondered if he should not have acted on the omen.

When the protector returned, he was not as convivial as he had been just one hour before; he seemed tense, angry, even bellicose. Without warning, he burst out and accused the men of treachery against his rule and alliance with the Woodvilles. Richard's wrath was directed especially at Hastings, who, among the three, had a special connection to his late brother's reign. After Edward's death, the king's favorite mistress, Jane Shore, had passed on to Hastings, and the liaison made Hastings' loyalty to Richard questionable. In his fury, Richard accused Shore of witchcraft, conspiring with the queen to cause one of his arms to wither. The accusation was incomprehensible to the counselors. Richard's arm had been withered since birth; besides, Elizabeth hated Jane Shore as only a wronged woman could, and surely would have chosen another accomplice if she had been foolish enough to stoop to witchcraft. The men were stunned.

Suddenly Richard's aides moved to restrain them. In the struggle, Stanley was struck on the side of the head and slid under a table, bleeding as he had in his nightmare. Morton was sent to the Tower; Stanley was allowed to remain under arrest in his own rooms. But Hastings was led out and immediately executed.

Stanley's sudden fall from power was a severe blow to his wife's plans. Deeply concerned over her husband's safety, Margaret realized that without his influence to shield her she could not proceed with her scheme to bring her son back to England. If Stanley was to be banished from court, she herself would be a virtual exile from the center of power. Her closest allies were the very men Richard had singled out for punishment. Only Buckingham, she thought, might one day be useful to her. For the time, at least, he remained in Richard's favor.

Even Jane Shore was not exempt from Richard's wrath. Shortly after Hastings' death, Richard forfeited most of her wealth, accumulated from years of fortunate liaisons, and sent her to prison. He persisted in his charge of witchcraft, but when nothing could be proved, shifted instead to charging her with being a whore. "Every man laughed . . . to hear it then so suddenly highly taken," Thomas More remembered,[17] but Richard would not be made a fool. He forced Thomas Kemp, bishop of London, to sentence Jane to the public penance of walking in a Sunday procession with a candle in her hand, dressed only in a white sheet. But she could not be humiliated. She blushed demurely and seemed even more attractive than she had before. Righteous women, flocking to see the harlot shamed, found they were moved to pity rather than censure. The men were enthralled.

Richard now turned his attention to the two heirs. Edward was in the Tower, but his brother had been allowed to join Elizabeth at Westminster. Richard's ally, Archbishop Thomas Bourchier, pleaded with Elizabeth to allow her son to join Edward. She was understandably reluctant, frightened by the rumors she had heard about Richard's plan to do away with the children to clear his own path to the throne. But the prelate's argument won her over. First he told her that the populace desired to see the young son of Edward IV, whose presence alone could quash disturbing rumors of dissension in the realm. Then he tried to convince her that the young king himself missed his close companion; she would deepen her child's grief if she refused to allow the two brothers to share each other's company.

Elizabeth was not fully reassured by these reasons, so Bourchier tried a more philosophical argument. Since her son was too innocent to have committed any crime, he told her, the boy had no need of sanctuary. She had nothing to fear as long as she believed that her son was guiltless. At last she allowed the child to go. "Farewell, my own sweet son; God send you good keeping," [18] she said, kissing the weeping child. She never saw him again.

With the children under his control and out of the sight of the sentimental populace, with his opponents eliminated or imprisoned, Richard moved to the next step of his plan. He was determined to convince the lords and commoners that the children of Edward and Elizabeth were, in fact, bastards and therefore unable to inherit the crown. He claimed that Edward had been betrothed to another woman before his marriage to Elizabeth — his brother's attachments to Eleanor Butler and Elizabeth Lucy, both noblewomen, made the accusation credible — making the Woodville marriage adulterous and the offspring illegitimate.

Using Buckingham as his mouthpiece, Richard presented the slander to the citizens of London in the Guildhall in late June. Then again on Sunday, June 22, the day on which Edward was to have been crowned, Dr. Ralph Shaa, a popular preacher, stood at St. Paul's Cross and repeated the fabrication to credulous masses, adding that Edward IV himself may have been an adulterous child of the dowager duchess of York: he never had looked much like his father. "This is," the speaker concluded, pointing each time to Richard, who made his appearance just at the final words, "the father's own figure; this is his own countenance — the very print of his visage, the sure undoubted image, the plain express likeness of that noble duke." [19]

The carefully staged performance, patterned after Edward IV's usurpation in 1461, was to have ended with a unanimous cry of "King

Richard! King Richard!" But for both Buckingham and Shaa the audience stood mute, "as they had been turned to stone, for wonder of this shameful sermon." [20] Buckingham was annoyed at the obstinate crowd and attempted to exhort them to acclaim the new king: Did they want Richard or not? But the listeners merely began to whisper to one another, still stunned. At last some of Buckingham's servants and Richard's henchmen, gathered together at the rear of the crowd, cried out for the proposed king and tossed their caps into the air. Buckingham, clutching at the opportunity, thanked the audience for their hearty and unanimous approval. The next day, he told them, he would lead them to request, as humbly as they might, that Richard take over the realm from the bastards.

Richard's plan was enacted so quickly, and was essentially so absurd, that the populace of London had no time to consider its real meaning for them. On June 25 Richard was asked to take the crown and modestly agreed. Before a great audience at Baynard's Castle, Buckingham again read the petition that awarded Richard the throne, this time to a more enthusiastic group of citizens. Richard then rode to Westminster and, at the moment that he first sat on the marble King's Bench, declared his reign begun. One June 26, 1483, Richard wrote later, "we entred into owre just title taking upon us oure dignities royall and supprane gouvernaunce of this oure royme of England." [21]

VII

The Rebel

Now that Richard had achieved his goal, Stanley, with his powerful associates and great wealth, was once again embraced as a loyal supporter. He became steward of the royal household, a position he had held under Edward IV, and was appointed by Richard to the Order of the Garter, an elite fraternity of noblemen that had been instituted by Edward III. Margaret Beaufort, too, was taken into the king's favor. For her coronation robes, she received ten yards of scarlet for her livery, six yards of crimson velvet for a long gown, six yards of white cloth of gold, six and a half yards of blue velvet, and six and a half yards of crimson cloth of gold for another gown. At the coronation ceremony, Stanley bore the king's mace. His wife carried the train of the new queen in a ceremony that was among the most elaborate ever staged in England.

Because of his precarious claim to the throne, Richard III knew that pageant and rite were essential to inspire awe in his subjects. He realized, as well, that threat of insurrection could not be ignored. From his captains throughout the land, Richard called for troops to protect him. The city of York, where Richard's support was especially strong, sent a contingent of soldiers each paid twelve pence per day for his participation in the events. Every man, however, was required to provide his own glove leather tunic, summer garb for the deflection of arrows and swords.

The number of troops astounded and even alarmed many onlookers. Some six thousand soldiers assembled with Richard on July 1, 1483, at Finsbury fields outside London, where the king-elect passed among them and thanked them for their presence. Then the huge procession made its way to the city. Many of the nobility, some of whom had once been staunch Lancastrians, prepared to kneel before the new king and his queen, Anne of Warwick.

The unfortunate Anne had seen her father, the failed King-Maker, fall at the hands of the Yorkists. When she was sixteen, she had been married to the son of Henry VI, but within a year found herself a widow when Edward was slain at Tewkesbury. Anne was a desirable heiress, despite her family's political affiliations, and in 1473 she was taken in marriage by Richard of Gloucester. Unlike Margaret Beaufort, who remarried in the same year, Anne seems to have had little choice in the selection of her husband. Dutifully, Anne presented Richard with a son, Edward, born at Middleham Castle in 1474. By the time she walked barefoot, as queen, upon a carpet of striped cloth, accompanying her husband to pray at St. Edward's shrine, she was already suffering from the consumption that, aggravated by personal sorrow, would soon kill her.

From the shrine, the sumptuously arrayed king and queen proceeded to the altar, where they would be anointed and crowned. Above Anne's head a canopy floated, with golden bells at each corner. She herself wore a coronet of gold and precious stones. Bishops flanked her. A mass of noblemen and noblewomen followed her. Perhaps none was so stirred by the ceremony as Margaret Beaufort. Listening to the long chorus of Latin songs, watching as the monarchs were divested of their robes and anointed, Margaret could not help but picture her own son receiving the crown to which he was heir. The Te Deum was sung, and at the offertory Margaret sat at Anne's left, kneeling in homage with her peers. There were many, kneeling just as she was at that moment, with as little good will toward Richard and as little loyalty to the Yorkists as Margaret herself felt. Her husband and the men he could easily sway, former supporters of Edward IV, the aides of her late second husband, Henry Stafford — all these would feel no remorse if Richard were deposed; all might be counted on to rally to her own cause.

Margaret also attended the coronation banquet, which began at four and lasted for five and a half hours, long even for medieval feasts. Her husband was among those who served the king from platters of gold and silver, which followed one another in seemingly endless succession. Each course contained numerous dishes — fish, fowl, meat, and game — spiced and sauced. Without forks, which had not yet been imported from the continent, diners could manage only minced, diced, or otherwise finely cut-up food, which they could pick up with their fingers or which would adhere to a chunk of bread. Recipes, whatever their basic ingredients, included unlikely combinations of spices, wine, and sweetening, sometimes effectively disguising rotting meats. Each course was preceded by a "subtlety," a sculpture in sugar depicting some historical or allegorical figure appropriate to the occasion. These were masterpieces of detail, and it is no wonder that chefs and their assistants were treasured members of any court's staff.

The opulence of the feast did not impress Margaret, whose asceticism extended to her eating habits. No one bothered to notice how little she ate and drank, how she turned away from the dripping fingers and greasy mouths of her dining partners. No one missed her when she departed early from the festivities to retire to the silence and solace of her rooms.

* * *

Within one week of the coronation, Buckingham realized his reward. In a grant soon endorsed by the first Parliament of the reign, he came into his inheritance of over £1000 per year and lands that included the manor of Amersham in Buckinghamshire; the Castle of Kimbolton in Huntingdonshire; Brecon, Hay, and Huntingdon castles in Wales; and three manors in Wiltshire. Besides this ample realm, he was made chief justice and chamberlain of North and South Wales and had the constableship, stewardship, and receiver generalship of the king's lands there. He used his own seal to raise troops, appoint officials, and assemble arms. In his own dominion, he was nearly as powerful as the king.

But he was not king, and perhaps he believed that he might have a chance — as much chance as Richard III had had — to take the crown. He believed that the easy acquiescence of the lords and commoners to Richard's stunning deception was caused, at least in part, by their fear of imminent civil war. Richard's forces were strong and well organized and ably commanded; the Woodvilles could boast no such army behind them, since Richard had taken many of Edward IV's finest troops with him.

Buckingham, warily watching the progress of Richard's reign, was convinced that it would end in doom. His own authority would be assured only if he sided with those who opposed Richard. Historians have speculated that Buckingham quarreled with Richard and angrily defected. But there seems little reason to have quarreled with a man who had handed him half a kingdom. Buckingham felt no loyalty to his monarch. He was a quintessential opportunist, and would follow power, wealth, and the lure of fame.

At Buckingham's stronghold, Brecon Castle, Bishop John Morton was kept as Richard's prisoner. There, Morton received an occasional visitor, Reginald Bray, a man Buckingham had no reason to suspect. Bray had been steward to Sir Henry Stafford and continued to serve Margaret. He was one of her most trusted business and estate advisers and soon became her political confidant. Unknown to Buckingham, Bray had used his visits to apprise Morton of Margaret's plans to secure the crown for her son. When those plans had been well thought out, Buckingham himself was gradually advised of them.

Realizing Buckingham's weak affiliation with Richard and his desire for ever more power, Morton and Bray led him into conversations that broached the delicate subject of rebellion. They found an attentive listener. Soon Buckingham knew as much as they wished him to know about a plan, already unfolding, to place a new king on the throne.

He learned that there were to be five uprisings across the south and west of England around the end of September 1483. At the same time, Henry Tudor was to sail from Brittany and lead a rebellion to defeat Richard. Buckingham was intrigued and saw reasons to believe that the rebellion, if under the correct command, could be successful. But he was not fully convinced that Henry Tudor, a man virtually unknown in England, could be placed on the throne.

One day as he rode to Shrewsbury, he met his aunt Margaret Beaufort on the road from Worcester to Bridgenorth. On her way to pay homage at the cathedral in Worcester, she stopped to talk with the young duke. Margaret knew from Reginald Bray that Buckingham was interested in her plan, and she knew, too, that he had some reservations. He had hinted to Morton and Bray that he, not Henry Tudor, was better suited to take the crown from Richard III. He was, after all, a well-known leader, the king's closest aide, and unquestioned ruler in a vast area of the country. Margaret Beaufort had no patience for this arrogance. She reminded him that both she and her son stood between him and the crown, that the plan in which he might be allowed to participate was of her devising and would not be taken over by a brash young duke. She assured him that she would see to it that her son won the throne to which he was entitled as a direct heir of Edward III through John of Gaunt, through John Beaufort, and through herself. If Buckingham had any doubts about the rebellion, they vanished after his conversation with Margaret. When he returned to Brecon, he defected from his king.

According to plan, Buckingham would lead "a great power of wild Welshmen" across the Severn from Wales into England. There, they would be joined by a contingent of other rebels ready to participate in the insurrection. But troops were difficult to assemble, and whatever mercenaries Buckingham could find were not sympathetic to any cause but the fattening of their own purses. They did not know why they were suddenly fighting the newly installed king and had no interest in the proposed usurpation. When the Severn flooded, leaving the troops without supplies, food, or the prospect of receiving the rest of their wages at the time promised, they scattered and fled, abandoning Buckingham to fight virtually alone. Even John Morton, realizing that the plan had — for a time, at least — failed, fled to his see at Ely.

Completely forsaken, Buckingham went into hiding. On October 15, 1483, he was officially proclaimed a rebel, and a hefty reward was offered to anyone who would turn him in. Bondmen would be set free; freemen would be given £1000. The reward was enough to cause one of his own servants, Ralph Banester, to betray his master to the sheriff of Shropshire.

> Base Banester this man was nam'd,
> By this vile deed for ever sham'd.
>
> "It is" quoth he "a common thing
> To injure him that wrong'd his king."
> Thus Banester his maister sold
> Unto his foe for hiere of gold . . .[1]

On all Souls' Day, November 2, 1483, on a new scaffold that Richard had ordered constructed, Buckingham was beheaded.

* * *

The insurrection has been thought proof that the two heirs by birthright to the legacy of Edward IV were already dead. The mystery of the "little princes in the tower" has inspired much historical debate. Were they dead? Who killed them? Some believe that Buckingham himself, though no stranger to murder, was appalled when he learned that the princes had died on orders from the king. He could not bear the idea that two innocent lives were sacrificed in one man's quest for power, and that deed itself turned him from support of Richard. But others argue that Buckingham may have been the murderer, acting on his king's orders, with little remorse.

The fate of the princes inspired many rumors. At the beginning of their imprisonment in the Tower, they were sometimes seen playing together on the grounds. Gradually, they were seen less and less frequently, and then not at all. They may have been killed, but it is just as likely that they were moved, perhaps far from London, where the sight of their boyish sporting could not evoke sympathy.

Not until the next century did a shocking story circulate about the princes. This version of their fate was told by Thomas More, who received his information directly from his mentor and guardian, John Morton. More insisted that his tale was based "not after every way that I have heard, but after that way that I have heard by such men and by such means as me thinketh it were hard but it should be true." [2] According to More, Richard III assigned one of his most trusted knights, James Tyrell, to do away with the children. Tyrell hired Miles Forest, "a fellow fleshed in murder," and John Dighton, "a big, broad, square, strong knave," to carry out the crime. One midnight, the two men stole into the boys' bedroom, quickly swaddled the children in their blankets, and pressed their feather pillows against their faces until "stifled, their breath failing, they gave up to God their innocent souls into the joys of heaven . . ." [3] Tyrell, after inspecting the bodies, ordered them to be buried under the stones at the foot of the stairs outside the White Tower. In 1674, two bodies were indeed found in a wooden chest below the stone staircase. Two and a half centuries later, the skeletons were examined by archeologists and appeared to be of two children, one about thirteen, the other ten. It was impossible to determine how long they had been buried. There is still no proof that the princes in the Tower were ever murdered, nor is there proof that Richard III killed them.

It may have been true, however, that after Buckingham's failed insurrection, Richard's personality underwent a profound change. He may have been shocked enough by the betrayal of his friend to mistrust everyone and fear for his own security. More maintains that after the princes were killed, Richard "never had quiet in his mind; he never thought himself sure. Where he went abroad, his eyes whirled about; his body privily fenced, his hand ever on his dagger, his countenance and manner like one always ready to strike again. He took ill rest a nights, lay long waking and musing, sore wearied with care and watch, rather slumbered than slept, troubled with fearful dreams, suddenly sometimes started up, leaped out of his bed and ran about the chamber; so was his restless heart continually tossed and tumbled with the tedious impression and stormy remembrance of his abominable deed." [4]

His worries, though, may have come not from his guilt but from external threats. Though Buckingham's rebellion had failed, word could not be brought quickly enough to Henry Tudor to keep him from fulfilling his role in the plan. The king, learning of the approaching danger from some of Buckingham's men, amply fortified Poole Harbor in Dorset. In mid-October, Henry Tudor sailed from Brittany, across the Channel, toward Poole. Intimidated by the ominous reception, he turned back at once. Richard's watch immediately sent word to the anxious king that the invasion had been thwarted. But Richard III knew that Henry Tudor would not remain in exile forever. Even if her son was frightened by the king's show of strength, Margaret Beaufort was not.

In January 1484 Richard took the drastic step of attainting Margaret Beaufort, "mother to the king's great rebel and traitor, Henry, earl of Richmond," asserting that she "conspired and committed high treason, especially by sending messages, writings and tokens to Henry, stirring him to come into the realm to make war; and has made chevisancez of great sums of money in the City of London and elsewhere to be employed in treason; and has conspired and imagined the destruction of the king and was asserting and assisting Henry, duke of Buckingham, in treason." Only because of Richard's abiding trust in Stanley was the punishment mitigated. "It is ordained and enacted," Richard declared, "that she shall be disabled in the law from having or inheriting any lands of name of estate or dignity, and shall forfeit all estates whatsoever, which shall be to Thomas Lord Stanley for the term of his life and thereafter to the king and his heirs. Any estate she has or are held to her use, of the inheritance of Thomas Lord Stanley, shall be void." [5] Stanley was ordered to keep his wife sequestered on his estates, away from accomplices with whom she could trouble the realm. While Richard openly asserted that Henry Tudor was "a Welsh milkesop, a man of small courage, and of lesse experience in martiall acts and feats of warre," he was clearly afraid of the young man's potential power — and especially that of his mother.

In effect, Richard was condemning Margaret Beaufort to exile within her own country, ordering her to be cut off from financial sources and political aid. Like Margaret of Anjou when she was forced to flee to France, Margaret Beaufort was to lose all power once she was deemed a pariah. Richard counted on Stanley's loyalty and Margaret's obedience both to her husband and to the king.

But Margaret had never been submissive to her husband, and she would take no orders from the king. Though she was not permitted to communicate with anyone, she assembled about her a small group of confidants with whom she continued her intrigues. Besides Reginald Bray, there were Christopher Urswick, a priest who served as Margaret's chaplain; an aide, Hugh Conway; and her personal physician, "a grave man and of no small experience," [6] Dr. Edward Lewis.

Lewis was most trusted. Even Urswick, who had been recommended by him, was told of Margaret's plot only "after an oath of him to be secret taken and sworne." Urswick was to bring messages to Henry in Brittany. Conway was to procure and deliver funds. Lewis was given the most delicate and vital assignments.

Before Buckingham's proposed insurrection, Lewis was sent to a powerful Welsh lord, Rhys ab Thomas, to effect a reconciliation between Rhys and Buckingham, a man Rhys saw as an interloper and tyrant in Wales. Without Rhys's support, it would have been impossible for any man to march troops through Wales; his own forces were strongly unified and powerful. Lewis was the one man who could successfully realize the reconciliation: he had been tutor to Rhys and remained a trusted friend. Lewis told Rhys nothing of the plan to bring Henry Tudor to England; only of Buckingham's role and the need for Rhys's cooperation. Even then, Rhys was suspicious of the project, until a brash act on the part of the king himself changed his mind.

Richard III, overly concerned with loyalty, especially from Wales, demanded a pledge of fidelity from Rhys and also insisted that he send his only son, Grufydd, as a hostage to the court. The keeping of hostages was not unknown, and the handing over of one's son was, indeed, the ultimate proof of loyalty from a subject. But Rhys declined to part with the child. He wrote to Richard that the five-year-old child was too young to leave his mother. His son, he continued, was "the onlie prop and support of my house nowe in being . . . And lastly, Sir, I may well call him the one half of myself, nay to speake more trulie the better parte of me, so that if your Majestie should deprive me of this comforte, I were then divided in my strength . . ." [7]

Rhys was annoyed at having been suspected of disloyalty, and Lewis' arguments seemed sensible. It was difficult to avoid falling under the spell of the glib physician. Described as "an active stirring man, of strong abilities," Lewis was a smooth orator. He was "a man of readie witt, cleare judgment, and well redd in the liberall sciences, as having had most of his breeding in Italie, in the universitie of Padua." [8] His patients included highborn ladies and gentlemen. One of those patients much interested Margaret Beaufort.

After her son's aborted attack on England, Margaret realized that extensive support would be needed when another landing was made. No longer could she rely on a commander like Buckingham if the troops were untrained and unruly. More important, she did not want the insurrection to begin yet another series of battles in an extension of the Wars of the Roses. She firmly believed that the Wars must at last be ended and that the surest way to effect any alliance between opposing sides was by a marriage. If Henry Tudor was to carry on the Lancastrian claim to the throne, he must be united with the Yorkists.

To that end, Margaret sent Lewis on a crucial errand. He was to visit a patient, Elizabeth Woodville, and obtain her cooperation and her support of Henry's insurrection. Not only did Margaret want the Woodville forces behind her son, she wanted Elizabeth of York, Edward IV's eldest daughter, betrothed to Henry. At last, Margaret believed, the red rose and the white would be joined, and the ugly Wars ended.

No one suspected that Lewis, when he visited Elizabeth at Westminster, came for any reason other than the health of the former queen. He did not tell her that he had been sent by Margaret Beaufort; he presented the plan as if it were his own. "You know verie well, madame," he told her, "that, of the house of Lancaster, the earle of Richmond is next of bloud, (who is living, and a lustie yoong batcheler,) and to the house of Yorke your daughters now are heires. If you could agree and invent the meane how to couple your eldest daughter with the yoong earle of Richmond in matrimonie, no doubt but the usurper to the realme should be shortlie deposed, and your heire againse to her right right restored." [9]

For Elizabeth, the plan offered the only hope of her release from virtual imprisonment. No one would ask for the hand of her daughter if her daughter were an outcast. However distasteful the "lusty young bachelor" may have been to her, Elizabeth immediately agreed to Lewis' proposal and suggested that he go, as a diplomat, to Margaret Beaufort to sound her out.

In Brittany, at the cathedral of Rennes, on Christmas morning of 1483, Henry Tudor swore that he would marry Elizabeth of York. His supporters, Lancastrians who had followed him into exile, knelt around him on the church pavement and paid homage to him as if he were already king of England. But a thorny path lay before him.

In August 1483, the French king, Louis XI, died. His heir, Charles VIII, a boy of thirteen, was weak and ill. The government was taken over by Charles's decisive older sister, Anne, wife of the lord of Beaujeu. Her foreign policies were to affect the welfare of Henry Tudor, still in exile in Brittany.

Anne was determined to conquer Brittany and incorporate the duchy into the kingdom of France. Though Duke Francis had managed to keep Louis XI at bay, he saw the dead king's daughter as a serious threat. More important, his aides feared the twenty-two-year-old woman. Especially influential was a former tailor who had risen to the position of treasurer, Peter Landois.

Landois wanted desperately for Brittany to remain independent and understood that the aid of England would be enormously valuable in the inevitable conflict with France. He approached Richard III with the plan to surrender Brittany's treasure — the hostage Henry Tudor — in exchange for England's support. Duke Francis, ill at the time of the secret negotiations, knew nothing of the betrayal.

But Lancastrians with Henry soon heard disquieting rumors. Word was sent to John Morton, then in Flanders, and soon Christopher Urswick, who was with him, was dispatched with a message: Henry must quickly escape into France. Henry then sent Urswick on to France, where he obtained permission for Henry to enter the country.

Landois, at the same time, was preparing to turn over Henry to the English who had been sent to retrieve him. Henry had to devise a plan that would enable both himself and the rest of his party to escape unharmed. He sent a group of supporters, led by his uncle Jasper, to pretend to seek out Duke Francis, then recovering in a town near the French border. Their progress would not be suspect, and they would soon be near enough to Anjou to cross over to safety. Henry, following later, set out on pretence of visiting an English friend not far from Vannes, where he had been living. Instead, he withdrew into a wood, disguised himself as a servant, and barely had crossed to France when Landois's men, suddenly suspicious, reached the border.

By October 1484, then, Henry found himself in France, protected by a regime he did well to distrust. He begged for aid — money, men, and ships — to sail to England, but the French had not yet decided whom to support. They wanted English aid to Brittany completely cut off and feared that Richard's negotiations with Landois might still achieve a solid pact, despite the loss of the hostage. For nearly a year, Henry in France and his mother in England were kept wondering about the fate of their plans.

Richard, meanwhile, saw many of his own hopes dashed. In April 1484, his only son and heir, eleven-year-old Edward, died. The following March his wife died, overcome with grief and weakened by tuberculosis. Now there was no royal heir and no hope of an heir. Rumors abounded that Richard intended to marry Elizabeth of York, his niece, and the talk reached even Henry Tudor. The loss of Elizabeth of York as a wife would have meant a severe blow to Henry's insurrection. It mattered to neither Henry nor his mother whether he married Elizabeth or her sister Cecily, who was mentioned in the bargain in case Elizabeth died before the marriage could take place. All that did matter was the union with a Yorkist, and Elizabeth, as the daughter of the still-beloved Edward IV, was by far the best choice. Henry Tudor well knew that many of his aides supported him only because he would one day bring a Yorkist to the throne.

Richard's suit of Elizabeth of York failed, and the king turned to the nobility in a last effort to gain the support he so vitally needed. He had never courted the nobility with favors and rewards. Unlike his brother Edward, he seemed not to realize that the support of the important magnates was continuously necessary. When he did bestow grants, he simply partitioned off lands that came into the royal holdings but usually had small value. In August and September of

1484, he gave several awards to those who had helped him in the retaliation against Buckingham. To Richard Radclyff "for his good service against the rebels" he gave Margaret Beaufort's land in Lincoln, which had a yearly value of £24; to Edward Brampton, lands in Northampton that brought in £20 a year; to John Pykeryng, land in Essex that earned slightly more than £26. When Richard finally decided on an heir, choosing John de la Pole, the earl of Lincoln and the son of his sister,* he bestowed Margaret Beaufort's estate on the twenty-year-old, property that was to revert to the crown when Stanley died.

Richard was more and more obsessed with the threat of insurrection and grew to believe that Henry Tudor was sure to succeed. He became publicly concerned with the usurper, attainted both him and his uncle Jasper, and warned the populace against the traitor:

> The . . . rebelles and traitours have chosyn to be there capetyne one Henry Tydder, whiche of his ambicioness and insaviable covertise encrocheth and usurpid upon hym the name and title of royall estate of this Realme of Englond, where unto he hath no maner interest, right, title, or colour, as every man ele knoweth; for his is discended of bastard blood bothe of ffather side and of mother side . . . And if he shulde atcheve his fals entent and pirpose, every man is lif, livelod, and goodes shulde be in his hands, liberte, and disposicion, whereby sholde ensue the disheretyng and distruccion of all the noble and worshipfull blode of this Reame for ever . . .

Richard asked that all his supporters rally to defend the throne against the usurper, and promised that

> our said soveraign Lord, as a wele willed, diligent, and coragious Prynce, wel put his moost roiall persone to all labour and payne necessary in this behalve for the resistence and subduyng of his seid enemys, rebells, and traitours to the moost comforte, wele and suerte of all his true and feithfull liege men and subgetts.[10]

Many surrounding the king were struck by his depression, which seemed to have begun in November 1483, after he had visited Exeter and was taken to a castle called Rugemont. He had once been told by a seer that when he came to Richmond, he would not have long

---

* The son, too, of the man Margaret Beaufort was once to have married.

to live. "Well, I see my daies be not long," he remarked on his return.

Richard III acted like a defeated man, and many of his subjects looked forward to a new king who would bring vigor, strength, and a renaissance of spirit to England. In Wales, the prophet and poet Robert of the Dale was already singing:

> Full well I wend,
> That in the end,
> Richmond sprung from Brittish race
> From out this land the Boare shall chace . . .[11]

VIII

Bosworth

True hope is swift and flies with swallow's wings;
Kings it makes gods, and meaner creatures kings.

RICHARD III, Act 5, Scene 2

IN 1485, the population of England numbered some four and a
half million. Of these, only twenty families made up the higher
nobility. A merchant class was rising, but poverty was endemic. Wan-
dering beggars roamed the roads and swarmed into London across
the only span that crossed the Thames, London Bridge. The nine-
hundred-fifteen-foot expanse of wood and stone was lined with four-
and five-story buildings, some arcading the roadway. Beneath the
bridge, oblivious of the turmoil of London life, thousands of swans
floated peacefully.

Beggars made travel perilous, and many who journeyed recited a
litany of rhymes: "A Charm Against Robbers," "A Charm Against
Thieves," "A Charm for Travellers." Some of the aggressive beggars
were poor students who found solicitation in fine English or Latin a
way of acquiring a small subsistence. Begging became so popular that
restrictions had to be enacted, and no scholar was allowed to beg on
the highways until the chancellor of the university duly determined
his poverty and provided him with a certificate. The student-beggars,
often armed with the swords they considered indispensable, were aggressive adolescents and were no less a threat to the innocent traveler
than were less educated vagrants.

Life was characterized by risk and danger, but also by gaiety,
exuberance, and a love of display. Those who could, tried to keep up
with the latest fashions, which by the late fifteenth century were extremely stylized. Padding was used to create wide shoulders for men's

abbreviated tunics, which reached only a few inches below the waist. Women's gowns were long, high-waisted, and often bore a flowing train. Most intriguing were the women's elaborate headdresses, so heavy that a small cap of wire netting beneath was necessary to lessen the discomfort and strain on the head. Shoes reached an absurdity in width and had broad, blunt toes, where only decades before they had had pointed toes curling so far up the leg that attachments were needed to prevent the wearer from tripping on his own feet.

Dress delineated class, and sumptuary laws were passed at intervals to prevent the lesser classes from assuming noble postures. In 1464, for example, no one below a lord or knight of the Garter — or his wife — could wear purple, cloth of gold, velvet, or sable; the fine for infraction was twenty marks. The wearing of satin or ermine by those of low estate was fined ten marks. An income of forty shillings a year was necessary to permit the wearer to sport scarlet cloth and any fur except lamb. The lower classes were doomed to cloth that cost less than eleven pence per yard, and girdles fastened with anything but silver.

The well-dressed man wore a shirt, breeches, short jacket, long coat, stomacher (similar to a jeweled cumberbund), hose, socks, and shoes. Shirts were edged with lace embroidered with silk, especially at the collar and cuffs. Women's cloaks were lined with exotic furs, and their gowns were fashioned of luxurious fabrics in jewellike colors: purple velvet, amber satin, crimson silk.

Under Edward IV foreign trade had become healthy, and cities were growing as the merchant class enjoyed a new prosperity. Castles throughout the countryside were allowed to deteriorate and fall into ruin, as affluent families moved to newly built manors nearer to the centers of trade. Soldiers behind cannon, replacing the famed English archers, had speeded the obsolescence of castle fortifications.

London itself was a vibrant metropolis. The banks of the Thames were lined with enormous warehouses for all manner of imported goods. There were three main merchant streets: Thames Street, with its fishmongers, ironmongers, vintners; Candlewick Street, famous for its cloth shops; and West Cheap, the finest street in the city, where the goldsmiths and jewelers were lodged. Many buildings were of wood, sometimes combined with stone. Only the newer structures used brick, made according to a technique learned from the Flemish. Churches and larger houses used glass imported from Burgundy or Lorraine,

Flanders or Normandy. Often, plain white glass was decorated with flowers or birds; for churches, figures of prophets were usual in glass ornamentation.

Streets were badly paved. Any rainstorm, however brief, flooded them, and rain was frequent. The mud became stagnant, and the stench was often overpowering. Some of the nobility, demonstrating their heightened sensibility, did not leave their homes without a fragrant pomander to carry before their noses.

Londoners, for all their commerce with Europeans, were fiercely English. Even Scotland, Ireland, and Wales were netherlands in their imaginations, and the inhabitants of those territories were nearly barbarians. The English despised Italians, wrote one sensitive visitor from Italy, treated them contemptuously, and often followed insults with assaults.[1] The highest compliment to a foreigner was that "he looks like an Englishman."[2] Antipathy to foreigners was caused by arrogance combined with fear. The English believed anything at home was necessarily better than anything continental; at the same time, they feared that all foreigners came to England plotting domination. "The English are great lovers of themselves, and of everything belonging to them," observed a Venetian visitor; "they think that there are no other men than themselves, and no other world but England."[3]

For all their haughtiness, however, the English inspired admiration. The anonymous Venetian found them handsome, well dressed, well built, and intelligent. They were polite, but the men, at least, seemed somewhat cold. The women had a reputation for being passionate, which caused intense jealousy among their husbands. "Although their dispositions are somewhat licentious," the visitor wrote, "I never have noticed any one, either at court or amongst the lower orders, to be in love; whence one must necessarily conclude, either that the English are the most discreet lovers in the world, or that they are incapable of love."[4]

The Venetian was especially struck by the lack of affection shown by English parents toward their children. Beyond the age of nine, most children were sent to be trained in another family's household, breaking ties with their parents at that tender age and being forced to render service to strangers. This seemed, to the visitor, an abomination. When he asked why the custom was perpetuated, he was told that the children might learn better manners away from their parents. But the Venetian thought privately that the English continued the practice out of their own greed. First, they would be served better by strangers' children than by their own, to whom they might show parental kindness. Moreover, he noticed that the English were "great epicures, and very avaricious by nature." They always saved the finest food for themselves, allowing their servants brown bread, beer, and on Sunday a ration of meat, which was to last the whole week. If children lived at home, they would have to share in the fine-milled white bread and spiced stews in which their parents so happily indulged.

The English were intensely concerned with the learning of manners and the placement of their sons and daughters in society, seeing their children as the most valuable of their possessions. From the time of birth, the child was swaddled, first physically and then psychologically, in an effort to ensure that there would be no balking against the strictures of custom. Childhood was not a time of idyll or reverie, but years of preparation for the serious enterprise of living as an adult. A youth was a man-child, dressed as a miniature version of his father and expected to try to emulate adults in all things. Both in his parents' home and later, when he became an apprentice in another household, the child was expected to conform and be docile.

> Reverence thy parents dear, so duty doth thee bind:
> Such children as virtue delight be gentle, meek and kind.

The parting of siblings and the estrangement from parents may have produced better soldiers and more stalwart widows. Sentimental loyalties were discouraged, and early devotion often was solely to one's nurse, rather than to one's blood relative.

Children learned early, by rote and by example, that few people could be trusted forever. Friends had constantly to prove themselves. Love, celebrated in poetry and song, was not prerequisite to the arranged marriages, which sent pubescent children to bed in order to join their fortunes.

If there were any one English obsession, it was money.

> Man upon mold [earth], whatsoever thou be,
> I warn utterly thou gettest no degree,
> Ne no worship abid with thee,
> But thou have the peny redy to tak to.

> If thou be a yeman, a gentleman wold be,
> Into sum lordes cort than put thou thee:
> Lok thou have spending, larg and plente,
> And always the peny redy to tak to . . .

If thou be a squire and wold be a knight,
And darest not in armur put thee in fight,
Then to the kinges cort by thee full tight,
And lok thou have the peny redy to tak to . . .[5]

Money was always on the mind of the merchant class. By late in the century the merchants of London were living in multistory dwellings with a ground-floor shop and warehouse and residence quarters above. The first floor usually consisted of a hall, kitchen, larder, and butlery. Additional stories contained bedchambers and parlors. Where the castles of nobility consisted of large chambers used for various purposes, the houses of the merchants were notable for their many small rooms: several bedrooms, parlor, wardrobes, servants' rooms, attic garrets, and the obligatory chapel.

The houses were heated by large fireplaces and lighted by candles. Furnishings were few. A bedroom would contain a featherbed, blankets, sheets, curtains, and perhaps a chest. If furnished elaborately, down pillows might be added, or a chair to supplement the bed for seating. In a "chamber for Straungers" the bed would always be made with a decorative coverlet. Wall hangings provided color and texture. Tapestries, woolen weavings, and skins adorned almost every whitewashed wall and covered tables and chests. Beds were surrounded by heavy draperies in brilliant patterns of scarlet, violet, azure, and gold. Floors were often strewn with rushes. If these were not frequently changed, all manner of debris accumulated beneath, sending up a troublesome stench.

Sanitation, in general, was primitive. There was only one municipal water system serving West Cheap, and although conduits were slowly added, most residents relied on well water for their needs. Only the wealthiest merchants had their own wells. Most of the houses had cesspits to accommodate solid sewage; liquid waste was emptied from buckets into gutters along the streets. Horse manure, accumulated in the stables behind the house, was carted away by a commissioned service and shipped to outlying areas to be used as fertilizer.

Outhouses were standard, with some families sharing a privy. Indoor facilities were considered shockingly unsanitary. Bathtubs were uncommon; the usual method of washing was in basins, a little at a time. But bathhouses, or "stews," were popular and were often confused with brothels, whose services they sometimes duplicated. There were several legitimate bathing centers scattered throughout London, a few exclusively for women.

Despite poor facilities, the English aspired to high standards of personal hygiene and paid a great deal of attention to their hair, skin, and teeth. *Regimen sanitatis salernitanum,* a Latin poem first translated into English in the fifteenth century, offered some rules for personal care.

> Rise early in the morne, and straight remember,
> With water cold to wash your hands and eyes,
> In gentle fashion rctching every member,
> And to refresh your braine when as you rise,
> In heat, in cold, in July and December.
> Both comb your head, and rub your teeth likewise . . .[6]

Teeth were cleansed with powders that might contain burned hartshorn or pulverized marble, myrrh, honey, and ground sage. Fragrant leaves were chewed as an antidote to halitosis, or the mouth would be rinsed with wine in which herbs had been steeped.

Hair was often dyed, and shining, curly tresses were the envy of most women. Steam baths were used to soften the skin, with emollients liberally applied. A lotion of Brazil-wood chips soaked in rose water was rubbed into pale cheeks to give them a rosy glow. If the complexion seemed too ruddy, root of cyclamen, ground into a powder, would be applied. Both men and women were concerned about freckles, moles, wrinkles, and warts, trying various mixtures of herbs, tinctures, or lotions to rid their skin of any blemishes. They were especially attentive to their feet, rubbing them with salt and vinegar to remove calluses, then applying a lotion of nettle juice and mutton fat or garlic, soap, and oil.[7]

Their concern with their bodies did not stop at the superficial. The *Regimen* was pithy in its advice:

> Use three Physicians still; first Doctor Quiet,
> Next Doctor Merry-man, and Doctor Dyet.[8]

All classes seemed prey to digestive upsets, and much of the *Regimen* consists of counsel on diets. In a word, the counsel was "temperance."

> Drinke not much wine, sup light, and soone arise,
> When meate is gone, long sitting breedeth smart:
> And after-noone still waking keepe your eyes.
> When mov'd you find your self to Natures Needs,
> Forbeare them not, for that much danger breeds . . .

Great harmes have growne, & maladies exceeding,
By keeping in a little blast of wind:
So Cramps & Dropsies, Collickes have their breeding,
And Mazed Braines for want of vent behind . . .
Great suppers do the stomacke much offend,
Sup light if quiet you to sleepe intend.
To keepe good dyet, you should never feed
Until you finde your stomacke cleane and void
Of former eaten meate . . .[9]

For indigestion and other ailments, garlic was thought to have multiple benefits. One could drink too much, eat too much, walk through the stench of the butchers' quarters in London, and be saved from dire consequences by eating garlic.

Beare with it though it make unsavory breath:
And scorne not Garlicke, like to some that thinke
It onely makes men winke, and drinke, and stinke.[10]

But even with garlic, certain precautions had to be taken against disease. Houses were to be situated away from stagnant water and sewage. Rooms should be light and airy, with as much ventilation as possible. Restful settings should be visited often: in the evening, grassy slopes and peaceful fountains; in the morning, the crisp air of mountains.

For the diseases that, despite all good counsel, worried every family, physicians had a meager offering of treatment. "Diet, drinke, hot baths, whence sweat is growing, / With purging, vomiting, and letting blood . . ." It hardly mattered what the symptoms might be; the treatment was the same. And it hardly mattered where the ailment might be lodged; the letting of blood was determined not by the condition of the patient, but by the season of the year.

Three speciall Months (September, April, May)
There are, in which 'tis good to ope a veine;
In these 3 months the Moone beares greatest sway,
Then old or yong that store of bloud containe,
May bleed now, though some elder wizards say
Some dayse are ill in these, I hold it vaine:
September, April, May, have dayes a peece,
That bleeding do forbid, and eating Geese,
And those are they forsooth of May the first,
Of other two, the last of each are worst.[11]

Beaufort coat of arms,
including the Tudor rose and portcullis
The British Library, Royal 19B xvii, f. iv

Pembroke Castle
*Royal Commission on Ancient and Historical Monuments
in Wales*

Edward IV, painter unknown
National Portrait Gallery, London

Richard III, painter unknown
National Portrait Gallery, London

Louis XI, after Fouquet (1415–1485)
*The Brooklyn Museum, Gift of the Estate
of Colonel Michael Friedsam*

Margaret Beaufort, painter unknown
*Portrait hangs in dining hall,
St. John's College, Cambridge*

Henry VII, painter unknown
National Portrait Gallery, London

Elizabeth of York, painter unknown
National Portrait Gallery, London

John Fisher, Bishop of Rochester, bust by Pietro
Torrigiano, sixteenth-century Italian sculptor
The Metropolitan Museum of Art,
Harris Brisbane Dick Fund, 1936

Margaret Beaufort, painter unknown
National Portrait Gallery, London

Man being helped into armor
The Pierpont Morgan Library

Battle of Barnet
University of Ghent

Musicians from fifteenth-century manuscript

Battle of Tewkesbury
University of Ghent

Execution of Edmund, Duke of
Somerset, uncle of Margaret Beaufort
University of Ghent

ue por enluminer / les cuers des refgardans
qui foit ocroifons / des biens des uergondans
pres fiet li efconfe / cefte pierre eft croiffans
enefie quamans foit / ₹ fecres ₹ celans
des biens damors vuet / eftre ours ₹ atendans

Henry VII, funeral effigy
Dean and Chapter of Westminster

Henry VII, effigy on tomb in
Westminster Abbey
Dean and Chapter of Westminster

Elizabeth of York, funeral effigy
Dean and Chapter of Westminster

Catherine of Aragon
National Portrait Gallery, London

Thomas More,
by Hans Holbein the Younger
The Frick Collection

Thomas Wolsey
National Portrait Gallery, London

Margaret Beaufort, effigy on tomb
in Westminster Abbey
Dean and Chapter of Westminster

Henry VIII and Henry VII,
by Hans Holbein, 1536–1537
National Portrait Gallery, London

Elizabeth I,
engraving by Crispin van de Passe the Elder,
after a drawing by Isaac Oliver, probably published as
a commemorative piece in the year of her death, 1603
The Folger Shakespeare Library

Though advice like that given in the *Regimen* was well known to the nobility and to the middle class, neither group wanted to give up their liberal dinners and abundant draughts of ale. The merchant class savored fine foods and liquors, copying the aristocracy in their food preferences, just as they copied the styles, colors, coiffures, and headdresses as far as they could, still complying with the strict sumptuary laws.

The merchants wanted to rise in society, and they wanted their neighbors to recognize their newly acquired status. They were intensely proud of their houses, the number of servants they employed, their carriages, and the sight of themselves passing through the streets. Even in death, they wanted to be noticed. Funerals became elaborate affairs costing grand sums. The hearse would be accompanied by dozens of blazing torches and a procession of lavishly garbed mourners.

The new gentlemen were concerned, too, with their heirs and their place in a new society. They began to send their sons to school. By the middle of the century there were six grammar schools, under Church auspices, where able young scholars could learn Latin. Gradually, the merchants began to prefer boarding schools, and many of their offspring were educated at Winchester and Eton. The intellectual life that had once been the sole province of the tutored aristocracy, now was taken up by the new middle class.

In 1476, an enterprising businessman returned to England from Flanders and decided to try at home a craft he had seen flourishing in Bruges. William Caxton set up the first printing press not far from Westminster Abbey and devoted his labors to the publishing of English works and translations of some popular religious and didactic tracts.

Caxton was born in 1421 in Kent and came to London as an apprentice to a mercer in 1438. The mercer died suddenly the next year, leaving his able assistant an ample bequest of £13. The sum was enough to enable any bright young man to live comfortably for a year, and Caxton took his legacy to Bruges, where he continued his apprenticeship, and then returned to London. He was accepted into the Mercers Company, a group that held a monopoly on the cloth trade and afforded its members a high position in the merchant class.

Again, he sailed to Bruges and there learned the art of printing, which had not yet been practiced in England. Few, in fact, had ever seen a printed book imported from the continent. But Caxton, believing that he could prosper with the new trade, set up a workshop at the sign of the Red Pale, near the chapter house of Westminster Abbey. His first book was ready in 1477.

The work was not, as might be expected, a printed Bible, but a compendium by a nobleman, Anthony, Lord Rivers, a brother of Elizabeth Woodville. *The Dictes and Sayings of the Philosophers* was followed by *The Recuyell of the Historyes of Troye* and *The Game and Playe of the Chesse.* Caxton's publishing advertisements were aimed at aspiring gentlemen. Virgil's *Eneydos,* he claimed, was "not for a rude uplandish man to labour therein but only for a clerk and noble gentleman." [12] Another volume was "not requisite for every common man to have, but to noble gentlemen that by their virtue intend to enter into the noble order of chivalry." [13]

He printed editions of Chaucer, Boethius, Lydgate, and John Gower. Especially with the works of Chaucer, which had been amended and elaborated since the fourteenth century, Caxton conscientiously tried to offer an accurate version of what the poet wrote, even going so far as to produce additional corrected printings if errors were pointed out to him.

In 1485, Caxton printed a fresh version of the tales of King Arthur and his legendary knights. Its author, Thomas Malory, had composed his *Morte d'Arthur* during a twenty-year prison term for assault, plunder of Coombe Abbey, rape, poaching, extortion, and jail-breaking, and had died at Newgate Prison in 1471.

But no matter. Malory's version of the tales celebrated courtly life and chivalry, and portrayed Arthur as the paragon of chivalric virtues. For his contemporaries, Malory urged a return to those higher values lost through centuries of brutal wars. The theme of the Holy Grail was subservient to the creation of the mythical Arthur, as if Malory knew intuitively that England needed and would respond to a grand hero, sweeping out of the west, to change the world.

* * *

Though Henry Tudor had spent half his life in Wales, he was not the white knight for whom England was waiting. Of medium height, pale complexion, with a long, lean, sober face, Henry was a quiet, introspective, thoughtful man of twenty-eight, whose early vicissitudes had shaped his personality. He had learned that he could trust only a few; that he could not make grand gestures, but instead take small, calculated steps; that he must be prudent, pious, and vigilant.

He did not know many Englishmen except the exiles who had

joined him on the continent, where he had spent all of his adult life. The English did not know him, and even those who looked forward to his return saw him more as a symbol of political unity than as a person. Henry Tudor, with his vow of betrothal to Elizabeth of York, would end the Wars, ascend to the throne, and lead England, all according to his mother's plan.

In 1485 it seemed that Margaret Beaufort's dream would be realized. Anne of Beaujeu finally decided in favor of supporting Henry, and gave him funds, a few ships, and several thousand men, at least a third of whom were French criminals. On Monday, August 1, he sailed from France toward England.

Henry had already written to some potential supporters, advising them of plans that his mother, John Morton, and Reginald Bray had carefully worked out. In Wales, John ab Meredith, a cousin of Owen Tudor's; Rhys ab Thomas; Thomas Stanley and his brother William; and Gilbert Talbot were all expecting his arrival. Bray had collected from the insurgent commanders a large sum of money to pay soldiers.

Just before sunset on Sunday, August 7, Henry and his motley troops landed at Milford Haven, the farthest extremity of South Wales. As he stepped on the land he had not seen for fourteen years, he knelt and kissed the shore. Then he led his army to Dale Castle, across the bay from his childhood home at Pembroke, easily overtook Dale, and spent the night there.

At dawn the next morning, with the village still shrouded in fog, Henry Tudor began his march. The army of Frenchmen, Bretons, and Welsh moved northward to Haverfordwest, reaching the crossroads town before noon. Then they headed over some thirty miles of difficult mountain paths, across the Prescelly Hills, into the parish of Nevern. Henry found no opposition from the Welshmen, who watched incredulously as yet another army pushed its way through their fields, but neither did he inspire any to drop their hoes and join his troops. On Tuesday, August 9, he marched through Cardigan and stopped for refreshment at an inn, the Three Mariners, before continuing along the coast to Llwynn Dafydd. He stayed there as a guest of Dafydd ab Ifan, whom he later rewarded with a drinking horn. On Wednesday, he stopped with Einon ab Dafydd Llwyd. On Thursday, at Mathafarn, he was said to have paused to consult a prophet and poet, Dafydd Llwyd ab Llywelyn. Dafydd's optimistic reading of the future came not from extraterrestrial influences but from the shrewd thinking of his wife, who told him to foresee victory so that if Henry became king, they should be rewarded; if he were defeated, she reasoned, they would not hear from him again.

Perhaps Henry believed Dafydd's prophecy the following day, when Rhys ab Thomas, whose allegiance had never been totally sure, agreed to support him. He brought with him the aid, too, of William ab Gruffydd and Richard ab Howell, and he arranged for herds of cattle to meet the army at Long Mountain so that the soldiers would be provided with victuals for their march ahead.

But as strong as Henry's support seemed, it lacked the outward demonstration of commitment by one man who had yet to communicate with Henry and whose aid was vital: his stepfather, Thomas Stanley.

Stanley's position was delicate. In July, when he decided to move supporters to Wales, he knew he would have to do so without arousing the king's suspicion. He told Richard that he was going to visit his estates in Lancashire. Richard did not fully believe him. He ordered him to leave his son, George, Lord Strange, as hostage; only then could he move freely. Richard, with George, then installed himself at Nottingham, nearly in the center of the country, where he could receive word on events wherever they occurred.

Some few years previously, during a conflict with Scotland, Edward IV had initiated a system of relaying dispatches to and from his troops. He stationed men on horseback at twenty-mile intervals along strategic roads. It was possible, then, for messages to travel a hundred miles a day, a swiftness hitherto unknown. Richard used that same postal system as he nervously awaited news. Stanley knew that any apparent defection from the king would be known quickly and would cost his son his life. Only Stanley's complete faith in his wife's plan allowed him to gamble for such high stakes. Lord Strange, understanding the risk involved, willingly stood as hostage while the rebellion unfolded, even when it seemed that his own execution would be inevitable.

By August 11, Richard had been informed that Henry had landed. But still he did not know the extent of his opponent's support in Wales, and believed that the powerful Welsh magnates would not allow Henry to pass unopposed. He counted on retaliation from Rhys ab Thomas, or even William Stanley, to stop Henry, and was shocked to learn that Henry had left Wales stronger and bolder than he had entered.

Lord Strange, after intensive questioning, finally confessed that both he and his uncle had contrived to help Henry by procuring support for him throughout Wales and England. He insisted, though, that his father knew nothing of the project, and offered to write to him requesting his return. Richard summoned Stanley back, threatening to execute his son if he did not immediately obey. Stanley had no reason to believe that Richard would not act on his threat, but he knew also that the time had come for boldness. He sent back word that he was ill and could not move.

Meanwhile, Richard had begun to organize his own troops and, putting off the execution of Lord Strange, left Nottingham for Leicester. By Sunday evening, August 21, the king's men and the usurper's troops were assembled on a plain some two miles south of Market Bosworth.

The opposing sides camped in uneasy silence, awaiting confrontation at daybreak. If Henry's foreign army did not know why they were fighting, and so could not be fully trusted, neither could the king's mercenaries. On the door of the duke of Norfolk's tent, under cover of darkness, a disgruntled soldier had written:

> Jack of Norfolk, be not bold,
> For Dickon, thy master, is bought and sold.[14]

But even if Richard had realized that he was already overcome, he could not have withdrawn or surrendered. A balladeer captured his spirit in lines penned after the fighting had ended:

> "Nay, give me my battle-axe in my hand, and the crown of England
> on my helm so high,
> For by Him that made both sea and land, King of England this day
> I will die.
> One foot I will never flee, whilst the breath is my heart within!"
> As he said so did it be. If he lost his life he died a king.[15]

A barrage of arrows began the attack, which soon turned to hand-to-hand combat. Though Richard had the larger force, Henry's men were well commanded and were amply fortified by the retinue brought — at the last moment — by his stepfather. Richard was moved to attack Henry, though he was surrounded by soldiers, and managed to slay William Brandon, the standard bearer, before he himself was cut down by a charge from William Stanley. The crown that Richard had worn into battle was hurled from his head in the struggle and landed in a hawthorn bush. Thomas Stanley retrieved it and placed it on the head of the victor. The king was dead. A new king reigned.

"Would you say that this was fortune?" Philippe de Comines asked in his memoirs. "No, no it was the judgement of God . . ." [16] "The realme of England hath this speciall grace above all other realmes and dominions, that in civill wars the people is not distroied, the townes be nor burned nor razed, but the lot of fortune falleth upon the soldiers, especially the gentlemen whom the people envy to too beyond reason: for nothing is perfect in this world." [17] The last battle in the long Wars had been fought, and England had survived.

IX

A Cheerful Strain

IMMEDIATELY, Henry issued a victory proclamation by circular letter, ensuring safe conduct to those who had fought at Bosworth and informing his subjects of the death of their former king.

> Henry, by the grace of God King of England and of France, Prince of Wales and lord of Ireland, strictly chargeth and commandeth, upon pain of death: that no manner of man rob nor spoil no manner of commons coming from the field, but suffer them to pass home . . . and moreover, that no manner of man take upon him to . . . pick no quarrels for old or for new matters, but keep the peace, upon pain of hanging . . .
>
> And moreover, the King ascertaineth you that Richard, Duke of Gloucester, late called King Richard, was slain . . . and brought dead off the field into the town of Leicester, and there laid openly, that every man might see and look upon him . . .[1]

Heralds read the letter throughout England, and many felt relief, even joy. The boar, Richard's badge, was removed from signs and torn from livery. The bloody body of the king, naked to gaping eyes, was proof again that the wheel of fortune had turned.

> . . . Now is the ffierce ffeeld foughten & ended,
> & the white bore there lyeth slaine;
> & the young Egle is preserved,
> & come to his nest againe.
>
> but now this garden fflourishes ffreshly & gay,
> with ffragrant fflowers comely of hew;

& gardeners itt doth maintaine;
I hope they will prove just & true.

our King, he is the rose so redd,
that now does fflourish ffresh and gay.
Confound his ffoes, Lord, wee beseeche,
& love his grace both night & day! [2]

Dafydd Llwyn Llywelyn ab Gruffydd celebrated the victory:

King Harry hath fought, and bravely done,
Our friend the golden crown hath won.
The bards resume a cheerful strain;
For the good of the world little R. was slain.[3]

English and Welsh bards came forth in a profusion of verse to commemorate both the battle and the romantic union of the white rose and the red.

As Henry rode south from Bosworth, his new subjects thronged to greet him. Cries of "King Henry! King Henry!" echoed across the countryside. In London, the mayor and aldermen staged a lavish welcome. They were dressed in purple velvet, and had called out the citizens to follow Henry's procession to St. Paul's. Henry's standards floated ceremoniously above the victors. On one, he displayed the red dragon of Wales, evoking not only his birthplace and ancestry, but the prophecy that Cadwalader, a valiant prince, would one day return and lead his people to victory.

After prayers and a Te Deum at the cathedral, the king celebrated, along with the whole of London. Plays, feasts, games, and music filled the ensuing days. The new king was particularly fond of music and would always include minstrels in his entourage to alleviate the tedium of the long and uncomfortable journey. And he was fond, too, of games: chess, backgammon, cards and dice, even tennis. He would give drama, especially mumming, an appreciative audience at banquets and court festivities.

One of the most delightful victory ballads survives in various versions. In "The Most Pleasant Song of the Lady Bessie," Humphrey Brereton, a servant of Margaret Beaufort's husband, Thomas Stanley, chronicles, not always factually, the plot to depose Richard, but makes Elizabeth of York, "littel Bessie," instrumental in bringing to England her dearly beloved "Earle Richmonde that prynce gaye . . ."

After hundreds of lines, the two are united when Bessie welcomes Henry back to London.

> Greate solas yt was to see,
>   I tell you, maysters, without lett,
> When the Reade Rowse of mekyll [great] price,
>   And yonge Bessie togeder were mett.
> A byshoppe them maryed with a rynge,
>   The two bloodes of highe renowne;
> Bessie said, nowe may we singe,
>   We two bloodes are made at one.[4]

Elizabeth of York was released from the Tower of London after Henry entered the city, but the forthcoming marriage was entered into cautiously. Henry was intent on making a smooth and sure accession to the throne, with no help from the Yorkists. He knew that his hereditary claim to the crown rested on controversial ground. Though the Beauforts had been legitimated by Richard II, some could still point to a clause, inserted later, that barred the family from royal pretensions. Henry decided to take the throne by acclamation and an act of Parliament.

Margaret Beaufort exulted in the cheers that followed her son to Westminster on October 29, 1485. The procession was no less than magnificent. Henry wore a doublet of cloth of gold and satin in green and white, the Tudor colors. Over it was draped a long gown of purple velvet, trimmed with ermine, laced and tasseled with gold. His charger was covered in trappings of cloth of gold, and a gold canopy was held above him, supported at each corner by four knights. Seven horsemen, wearing crimson and gold, followed; henchmen and footmen wore the Tudor colors. Heralds and trumpeters, glittering in their gilt costumes, streamed through the streets. London burst forth with the red rose on buildings, walls, and gates. The crowned portcullis, from the Beaufort badge, appeared on pennants and banners. Finally Archbishop Bourchier, assisted by Bishop John Morton, anointed and crowned Henry VII.

No one was more joyful about the advent of the new king than Margaret Beaufort. Finally, at forty-four, she had realized her only dream: to see her son claim his rightful inheritance. Henry's return, his triumph, was the pinnacle of her life. She saw in him not only the culmination of the Beaufort line, but the beginning of a new dynasty for England, one that would reign without the taint of war and dissension. What Margaret of Anjou had attempted to do in decades of bloodshed, Margaret Beaufort had achieved by nearly fifteen years of delicate diplomacy and one swift battle.

* * *

The fifteenth century was often a deeply pessimistic one, and fortune's fickleness seemed a hazard to everyone. The highly placed could fall into shame; the lowborn could plummet into abject poverty. As poets plied the theme, a turn of fortune's wheel meant eventual tragedy for those whose station seemed enviable and secure. Never did the wheel seem to turn for the better.

> Thys warlde ys varyabyll,
> No-thyng ther-in ys stable,
>   A-say now, ho-so wyll.
> Syn yt ys so mutable,
> how shuld men be stable?
>   yt may not be thorow skyll! [5]

When Margaret Beaufort watched her son become king, she thought of the three kings she had seen fall: Henry VI, by his own mishandling of the onus of kingship; Edward IV, by his frivolous dissipation; Richard III, by his fateful miscalculations. She remembered the misfortunes of her own father and of her guardian, the earl of Suffolk. She knew that her son had been able to triumph only after another woman and her son, Margaret of Anjou and Edward, had failed. She believed that Henry was close to her in spirit. Because he had been disillusioned early, as she had, he would live with disillusion for his entire life. She sensed in her son a calm and an integrity that previous monarchs in her lifetime had not had.

> Musyng uppon the mutabilite
>   off worldye changes & grett unstableness,
> & me remembering howe grett adversite
>   I have seen fall to men off highe noblenes —
>
>   furst welthe, and then egeyn distres,
>   nowe uppe, nowe downe, as fortune turnethe hur whele,
>   Best is, me thinke, for mannys sikernes
>   to trust In god & labour to doo well.
>
> Wee nede not nowe to seke the cronicles olde
>   off the romans, nor bockas tragedye,

to rede the ruyen & fallys manyffolde
off prynces grett, putt to dethe & myserye
In sondrye landes, for wee have hardelye
here In thys lande with-In the xx yere
as wonders changes seen before our eye
as ever I trowe before thys any were.[6]

Henry was careful about those to whom he gave his trust and generous with those who had proven their loyalty. One of his first acts as king was to grant a pension to his old Welsh nurse. Quickly, he lifted the attainders on his mother; his uncle, Jasper Tudor; Edward Stafford, the young son of the late duke of Buckingham; and Elizabeth Woodville.

Now in control of her own property, Margaret found her wealth and influence to be considerable. Her son augmented that wealth by grants made in the first two years of his reign. On August 3, 1486, he gave his mother the wardship of Edward Stafford and his brother Henry, worth five hundred marks per year. In addition, she received £1000 per year out of the lordships of Holderness for the children's "governaunce and supervision." On October 11, Henry made a grant "for life to Margaret Beaufort of the right of nomination and appointing the steward, receiver, bailiff, parker and all other officers within the king's lordship of Ware, Co. Hertford." She chose the faithful Reginald Bray as her steward general; other officers were picked from among Henry's supporters at Bosworth.

On March 22, 1487, Henry issued a grant for life to his mother of castles, lordships, and manors in many areas, including Devon, Somersetshire, Hertfordshire, Derbyshire, Yorkshire, and Northamptonshire. The generous grant comprised some fifty valuable properties.[7]

Not only were grants made that would provide her with income; land was given in her name to religious orders. On March 12, 1486, at Margaret's special request, a grant was made to one William, abbot of the monastery of Ss. Peter and Paul at Bourne, County Lincoln, for a nearby manor and its property.

Jasper was created duke of Bedford, and in the fall of 1485 married Katherine Woodville, twenty-eight, the widow of the duke of Buckingham and the youngest sister of Elizabeth Woodville.

Stanley was most amply rewarded for his support at Bosworth. Estates between Manchester and Bury, and in several sites in Lancashire, were added to his already large holdings. At the end of October

1485 he was created earl of Derby. In March 1486 he was made constable of England, high steward of the duchy of Lancaster, and constable of Halton Castle, Cheshire. His son George, Lord Strange, the eldest surviving son of his first marriage with Eleanor Neville, was rewarded for his loyalty by being made a knight of the Garter and a privy councilor.

John Morton, returned from exile to attend the coronation, became chancellor of England in March 1486 and toward the end of that year acceded to the post of archbishop of Canterbury. In 1493 he became a cardinal. He was a close adviser to the king, especially helpful in matters of finances. He was said to have devised a foolproof method of procuring funds from Henry's subjects, "persuading prodigals to part with their money, because they did spend it most; and the covetous, because they might spare it best; so making both extremes to meet in one medium, to supply the king's necessities." [8]

Reginald Bray was created a knight of the Bath, and then a knight of the Garter. He was appointed constable of Oakham Castle, member of the privy council, high treasurer and chancellor of the duchy of Lancaster. An architect as well as a statesman, he designed the chapel of St. George at Windsor Castle and Henry's private chapel at Westminster, where the royal family would someday be buried.

In January 1486, five months after his reign began, Henry at last married Elizabeth of York. Despite Humphrey Brereton's romantic ballad, the two had not been lovers before Henry went into exile. Elizabeth was just six years old then, and most probably never saw Henry. In the first months of his reign, Henry became acquainted with the woman his mother had chosen to be his wife and seemed to find her congenial.

Proof of her fertility may have postponed the marriage for those months, a delay that has long puzzled historians. While Elizabeth, as a Yorkist, had been extremely useful in enabling Henry to claim the throne, she would be far less useful if she was unable to begin the dynasty of which Henry and his mother dreamed. By the time the nuptials were performed, Elizabeth was probably already pregnant. The populace of England, almost giddy over the romance, looked forward to the royal marriage.

Because the pair were distantly related, a bull was issued by Pope Innocent, sanctioning the marriage. A Latin epithalamium was written to commemorate the event, and an anthem was sung, concluding:

God save king Henrie, whereso'ever he be,
And for queene Elizabeth now pray wee,
And for all her noble progenye;
God save the church of Christ from any follie,
And for queene Elizabeth now pray wee.[9]

The nuptial feast was appropriately elegant. A first course of twenty-three dishes included hart, pheasant, swan, capons, lamprey, crane, pike, heron, carp, kid, perch, mutton, custard, tart, and fruits. A subtlety was then brought out for the admiration of the diners, accompanied by the singing of ballads. A second course included peacock, cock, partridge, sturgeon, rabbit, egret, quail, lark, venison, quince, cold baked meat, and concluded with another subtlety and another round of songs.

Guests — except for the ascetic Margaret Beaufort — relished the elaborately sauced and spiced dishes. Venison was cut into strips and cooked in a sauce of milk, egg yolk, sugar, and salt. Soups were made of ground almonds, beef or fish broth, sweet wine, ground capon, milk of almonds and sugar. There were stews of chopped roast pork, fried onions, beef broth, pepper, cinnamon, cloves, and mace; of capon, strong wine, cinnamon, pine cones, sugar, cloves, almonds, ginger, salt, and saffron. Some of the pulpy mixtures were poured into a pastry shell, covered with dates and raisins, glazed with egg yolk, and baked.

For display, a peacock was cleaned, roasted, then arranged on a platter with its feathers fanned open. The top half of a capon was sewn to the bottom half of a pig, and the whole stuffed with eggs, bread crumbs, salt, saffron, pepper, and suet. The "cokyntryce," as it was called, was then roasted on a spit, basted with egg yolk, powdered ginger, and saffron. Sweets, fruits, and nuts followed, with some diners preferring hard cheese, supposed helpful in preventing constipation.

The feast itself was conducted according to rigid prescription. Servants had been instructed from a manual, "How to Serve a Lord," that permitted no deviation. Tablecloths and napkins were "clenely clene and redy according to the tyme." Basins for the rinsing of greasy fingers, pitchers, platters for bread, spoons, saltcellars, and carving knives (for suckling pig or whole roast kid) were on hand. The dishes were served in strict order, with heron following crane, and rabbit following pigeon, not the reverse.

The sovereign was served first from a dish of silver or gold plate. Then the guests were given their fare, "after ther degree." When the meal was ended, three or four hours after the first platter was borne to the table, the staff had to take up "all manner of thynge," including the trestles and stools that had served as banquet tables and seats. They were hardly done before requests came for bread and wine, the "all night," to stave off hunger until morning. This small repast was offered on bended knee to knights and ladies.[10]

* * *

After the wedding feast Margaret accompanied Elizabeth to the king's residence at Winchester, where the bride was to spend her confinement. Winchester Castle was chosen because it was said to have been built by King Arthur, and Henry had decided that his firstborn must be steeped in tradition.

From the moment of the marriage, Margaret took over the running of the household in every detail, composing her "Ordinances as to what preparation is to be made against the deliverance of a queen as also for the christening of the child of which she shall be delivered." The edict left nothing in doubt. Margaret saw to it that Elizabeth's chamber was arranged according to traditionally accepted modes of confinement. The queen was quite literally confined. Her room had only one window through which light and air could enter. All other windows were hung with thick cloths. When the birth was imminent, the young mother was kept from any visitors except the women who would see her through the delivery. She was permitted no visits at all from men.

The birth was explained as having come several weeks earlier than expected, and all the court whispered fearfully over the fate of what they thought was an eighth-month child. Superstition held that the eighth month was more precarious for birth than the seventh. But the child, born on September 19, 1486, was a healthy, fair-haired boy. Henry Tudor gave his heir the evocative Welsh name of Arthur. "Yet some men say in many parts of England that King Arthur is not dead," Malory had written, "but had by the will of our Lord Jesu into another; and men say that he shall come again . . ."

The child's birth was magnificently celebrated. Trumpeters and minstrels paraded through the streets, and poets sharpened their nibs.

"I love the rose both red & white."
"Is that your pure perfite appetite?"
"To here talke of them is my delite!"
"Joyed may we be,
oure prince to se,
& rosys thre!" [11]

With Henry the red rose and Elizabeth the white, Arthur was dubbed the "rosebush of England," from whom the new Tudor line would emanate.

Margaret Beaufort immediately took charge of her grandchild's care, a task that was more pleasure than duty. Elizabeth developed an illness after the birth; it has been described as ague[12] but may have been related to a strange outbreak in the fall of that year.

A newe kynde of sicknes came soldenly through the whole region . . . which was so sore, so peynfull, & sharp that the lyke was never harde of, to any manes remembraunce before that tyme: For sodenly a dedly burnyng sweate invaded their bodyes & vexed their bloud with a most ardent heat, infested the stomack & the head grevously: by the tormentyng and vexacion of which sicknes, men were so sore handled & so painfully pangued that if they were layed in their bed, beyng not hable to suffre the importunate heat, they cast away the shetes & all the clothes lying on the bed.[13]

Two mayors of London succumbed to the disease within a few days, and some citizens, seemingly recovered after twenty-four hours, relapsed once, or even twice, and then died. Physicians were perplexed but eventually came upon a method of treatment: lukewarm baths, moderate heat, moderate covering. Absolute rest for twenty-four hours was required.

For new diseases or old, physicians' remedies were few and their methods of diagnosis even fewer. Most diagnosis was made by analysis of urine, with color being matched to the gradations on an annotated chart. Red urine signified fever; pale urine meant indigestion; saffron-colored urine indicated jaundice; thick, reddish, milky urine signified gout. Instructions to physicians directed their eye to the various attributes of a urine sample that could indicate the presence of disease; the examiner had to be aware of color, texture, sediment, froth, and, of course, the appearance of blood.

Too much blood was believed to be the cause of much disease, and blood-letting was consequently a much-used treatment. Blood-letting was thought to effect wondrous results: it would clear the brain, strengthen the memory, purify the stomach, sharpen hearing, dry tears, dispel anxiety — even produce a musical voice.[14] But physicians were cautioned that blood-letting must be done with care, and always according to certain indications of the calendar, corresponding to signs of the zodiac. Ideally, certain incisions were not to be made at all in certain months; ideally, blood-letting should be done at the new moon. But medieval physicians rarely worked under ideal conditions.

Gradually, with little medical intervention, the strange sweating-sickness of 1486 abated, but it was, predictably, seen as a sign "that kyng Henry should have a harde and sore beginning, but more truly . . . it pretended & signified that kyng Henry to the extreme poynte and ende of his naturall life should hever have his spirite and mynde quyet . . ." [15]

The infant was protected, as far as possible, from the disease. Arthur saw little of his mother but spent his days in the wooden cradle, some forty-five inches long and twenty-two inches wide, that his grandmother had ordered for him from the court's carpenters. The frame was elaborately painted, and it was lined with cloth of gold, ermine, and crimson velvet. Three women were assigned to care for him: Elizabeth Darcy served as mistress, Agnes Butler and Emlyn Hobbes as rockers. Each was paid a bit over thirty-three shillings for half a year. His grandmother, guided by a physician, prescribed and ordered his nurses' diet and provided for tasters to sample the dishes before they were served to the women who suckled the prince.

The baptism was likewise prescribed in detail by Margaret. Arthur was to be given a small candle to carry to the altar. Two hundred torches were to be carried in procession before the infant; twenty-four were borne by squires. The torches were lighted after the ceremony; then the candle was lighted and presented by the child at the altar, with the king's donation to the church.[16] Thomas Stanley stood as godfather to his wife's grandson. Elizabeth Woodville, the mother of the queen, stood as godmother.

Though Margaret was supreme in the household of Henry VII, she could no longer control and manipulate political affairs as she had before Bosworth. Henry was indeed condemned to a life in which his spirit and mind could never rest. From the first days of his reign, he was concerned with security, and created a special contingent of fifty men, the yeomen of the guard. Half were armed with bows and arrows, the others with a new weapon, the harquebus, an innovation in forearms; it was ignited with a match and in shape was suggestive of a crossbow.

The position of yeoman was not new, but Henry's transformation of the office to that of personal bodyguard had no precedent. Edward IV's yeomen had been servants and valets, twenty-four of the "most semely persones, clenely and strongest archers, honest of condicions and of behavoure, bold men, chosen and tryed out of every lordes house in Ynglond for theyre cunning and vertew. Thereof one to be yoman of the robes, another to be yoman of the wardrobe of beddis in houshold . . . another to be yoman of the stole . . . another to be yoman of the armory; another to be yoman of the bowes for the king; another to kepe the kinges bookes; another to kepe his dogges for the bowe . . ." [17] Apparently the requirement that they be able soldiers was made only to weed out any who might be disloyal. Though they were sometimes sent out as ambassadors or to aid in arrests, their duties were domestic rather than military. They did not need special strength to deal with Edward's pet dog. The larger animals, lions and leopards, which were sometimes received as gifts from foreign rulers, were kept in a zoo in the Tower.

Henry's yeomen were to guard the king day and night, permitting no one who appeared suspicious to gain access to him. They acted as the king's messengers and general servants, and kept watch outside his bedchamber, making a search every fifteen minutes for arson, noise, treachery, threats — in short, anything that might harm the king.

They had special uniforms of white and green, damask jackets embroidered front and back with vine branches, decorated with silver and gold spangles. Central to the decoration was a red rose. Though the yeomen were strong, brave, and loyal, they could not forecast or prevent insurrection, or stop the progress of a pretender to the throne.

In May 1487, Lambert Simnel, a ten-year-old student of Richard Symons, a priest, claimed to be Clarence's son, Edward, the earl of Warwick, and therefore the rightful heir to the crown. Symons taught his charge well and then took him to Ireland, where he knew the nobility were unsympathetic to Henry. On May 24, in Dublin, Simnel was crowned King Edward VI.

Not even the remaining loyal Yorkists, who still waited for a chance to overthrow the king, believed that Simnel was the true heir. But they were willing to use his presence as an excuse to begin a rebellion.

With the support of Edward IV's sister Margaret, the duchess of Burgundy, they assembled troops and met in battle with the king's forces on June 11, near the town of Stoke.

The Yorkist troops, reinforced by German mercenaries, were formidable opposition to the Tudor army, but the king was triumphant. Both Symons and Simnel were captured, but neither was executed. Believing Simnel to be essentially harmless, Henry pardoned him and gave him a small position in the royal household, first in the kitchen, then as falconer. The dissident Yorkist captains were slain. The lands of the earl of Lincoln were given over to the king's mother.

The king had survived more than two years of his reign when the Simnel affair was suppressed. Finally, Henry decided to crown his queen. The delay in the coronation may have been due partly to the queen's pregnancy and recovery from her subsequent illness, but that would not have postponed the ceremony for two years. There may have been another pregnancy, perhaps ended by miscarriage, which prevented Elizabeth from appearing in public. Or perhaps Henry waited, vigilant as ever, to be sure of his own power as king before he made a prominent display of his Yorkist wife.

On November 24, 1487, Elizabeth left her suite at the Tower and made her way to Westminster. Her train was carried by her sister Cecily. Henry's uncle, Jasper, rode as grand steward. Lord Stanley was high constable. The next morning she walked upon the traditional carpet of striped cloth to Westminster Abbey. A crowd pressed so close to see her and to snip off portions of the carpet as a remembrance that several were trampled to death. The king and his mother, allowing Elizabeth sole grandeur on her day, watched the coronation from behind the latticework of a private box.

Again at the coronation feast, while throngs of noblemen gorged on a lavish banquet, Henry and Margaret sat together at the rear of the hall, hidden behind a screen. The next day, when the queen heard mass at St. Stephen's Chapel, her husband was with her, and her mother-in-law was beside her. Their prayers were for England.

X

Of Virtue Rare

MARGARET BEAUFORT rose daily at five and began to pray. She said matins with one of her gentlewomen, then again, alone with her chaplain. She heard four or five masses each day, kneeling until her back throbbed with pain. She ate no breakfast and only a frugal dinner, unless it was one of the fast days, all of which she rigorously kept. Throughout the day she returned to the altar, said dirges and commendations, evensongs and psalms. At night, in her private chapel, she again prayed. At confession, which she made every third day, she wept copiously. At ceremonies and celebrations, onlookers were struck by her outpouring of tears.

Several times each week she wore hair shirts or girdles of hair, sometimes one and sometimes the other. Often her skin was pierced and raw from the abrasive cloth. When she was in her mid-fifties, with her husband very much alive, she obtained Thomas Stanley's permission to take a vow of chastity, and lived out the remainder of her life in celibacy.

> In the presence of my Lord God Jesu Christ & his blessed Mother the glorious Virgin St. Mary & of all the whole company of Heaven & of you also my Ghostly Father I Margaret of Richmond with full Purpose & good Deliberation for the Weale of my sinfull Soule with all my Hearte promise from henceforth the Chastity of my Bodye. That is never to use my Bodye having actuall knowledge of manner after the common usage in Matrimonye . . . & now eftsence I fully confirm it as far as in me lyeth beseeching my Lord God That He will this my poor wyll accept to the Remedye of my wretched Lyfe & Relief of my sinfull soule and that He will give me his Grace to perform the same . . .[1]

At Hatfield, one of her manors, she kept twelve poor aged men and women, providing them with food, lodging, and clothing, nursing them if they became ill and burying them when they died. Strangers were welcome. Food and drink were denied to no one. Her servants were treated fairly, and any grievances they had were dealt with immediately. Her households were paragons of efficiency, with written ordinances read four times a year and instructions handed down in minute detail.

Her supervision of the king's family included even her son's bedchamber, for which she issued a doctrine regarding the making of his bed. A yeoman was to bring in the bedclothes, draw the curtains, and an usher was to hold the curtains together. Then two squires were to position themselves at the head of the bed and two yeomen at the foot. The bedclothes were to be laid on a carpet. A yeoman was to leap onto the bed, jump up and down, beat the featherbed into airy softness, and smooth it evenly. After the mattress was thus prepared, the sheets were to be laid and the pillows arranged precisely as the king wanted them. Last, holy water was sprinkled on the bed. All that accomplished, the yeomen and squires were advised to partake of the refreshment that had been readied for them: meat, bread, ale, and wine, and "to drinke all togeder goodly."

Margaret allowed no detail to be overlooked. Whenever Elizabeth withdrew for the birth of a child, Margaret had removed from the queen's bedchamber all tapestries with representations of human figures so that during Elizabeth's labor she did not become frightened by "figures which gloomily glare." [2]

With her own penchant for hair shirts, it was understandable that Margaret looked with disdain at the elaborate fashions of her contemporaries. She herself dressed in somber colors, though in her youth she had been seen at festivities in gowns of crimson or shimmering cloth of gold. Her scorn of the flamboyant styles was especially directed toward funeral apparel, and she composed a special ordinance for the "reformation of apparell for princesses and great estates with other ladies and gentilwomen for the tyme of mornyng . . ." These ordinances prescribed the size of the mantle, the form of the gown, the length of the train for the greatest estates, the lowest, and all gentlewomen in between. Only one other lady was allowed to wear apparel as sumptuous as that of the queen: the king's mother.

Besides religious devotion and the supervision of domestic affairs, Margaret Beaufort again had time for scholarly pursuits. She was a patron of William Caxton and his successor, Wynkyn de Worde, both of whom published books at her request. Among the works she sponsored were *A Treatise Concerning the Fruitful Sayings of David, King and Prophet,* Henry Watson's translation of *The Great Ship of Fools of This World,* and William Atkinson's translation from Latin of the first three books of *The Imitation of Christ.* This last work she wished she could have translated herself, but she did not have sufficient classical background.

She did, though, translate *The Mirror of Gold for the Sinful Soul.* The tract was written for perpetual penitents like Margaret, "to the extent that the synfull soule, sayled and defouled by synne, maye, in every chapitoure, have a new mirroure, wherein he may beholde and consider the face of his soule." The seven chapters, one for each day of the week, dealt with the filthiness and misery of man, sins in general and their effects, penance, ways to flee from the world, false riches and vanity, death, and the joys of paradise countered with the pains of hell.

William Caxton was so grateful for Margaret's patronage, no small aid for the precarious enterprise of publishing, that he dedicated to her his printing of *Blanchardine and Eglantine,* which appeared in 1489.

> Unto the right noble puyssaunt and excellent pryncesse my redoubted lady my lady Margarete duchesse of Somersete, moder unto our natural and soverayn lord and most crysten kynge Henry the seventh by the grace of God kynge of englonde and of ffraunce lord of yrelond etc. I, Wyllyam Caxton and his most indigne humble subgette and lytil servaunt present this lytyl boke I late receyved in ffrenshe from her good grace and her commaundement wyth alle, for to reduce and translate it in our maternal and englysh tongue, whiche boke I had longe fore solde to my sayde lady and knewe wel that the storye of hit was honeste and joyefull to all vertuouse yong noble gentylmen and wymmen for to rede therin as for their passe tyme, for under correction in my jugement hystoryes of noble fayttes and valyaunt actes of armes and warre which have ben achyeved in olde tyme of many noble prynces, lordes and knyghts, as wel for to see and knowe their walyauntnes for to stand in the specyal grace and love of their ladyes. And in lyke wyse for gentyle yonge ladyes and damoysellyes for to learne to be stedfaste and constant in their parte to theym that they one have promysed and agreed to such as have put

> their lyves ofte in jeopardye for to playse theym to stande in grace . . .

The book dealt with the love of Prince Blanchardin for the Princess Eglantyne

> And of the grete adventures, laborous anguysshes, and many other great dyseases of theym both to fore they myghte atteyne for to come to the finall conclusion of their desired love . . .[3]

As for Margaret, she had only one love. She addressed Henry VII as "my oune suet and most deere kynge and all my worldly joy." Doubtless much of her praying was on her son's behalf. "Our Lord gyve you as longe good lyfe, helthe and joy, as your most nobyll herte can dessyre, with as herty blessyings as our Lord hath gevyn me power to gyve you."[4] "My derest and only desyred joy yn thys world," she wrote on another occasion and ended her letter, written on his birthday, "At Calais town thys day of Seynt Annes, that y dyd bryng ynto thys world my good and gracyous prynce kynge and only beloved son."[5]

Several Tudor historians tried to explain the uncommon phenomenon of Margaret's having had three husbands and only one child. In their ardor to glorify their king, some postulated that after having given such a gift to the world, there was no need for God to bless Margaret with any more children. But bearing a child when she was only an adolescent herself, a frail, thin, and small girl, may have made it impossible for her to bear any more children. It is unlikely that she had tried to prevent another pregnancy, since birth control was violently condemned by the Church. Even if she had, she would probably have failed.

Methods of contraception were often far removed from the site of conception and remained steeped in superstition. Various herbs were thought to be effective, and women tried teas of marjoram, thyme, parsley, lavender, or leaves from fruitless trees to induce sterility. Brides wore wreaths of rosemary or myrtle next to their breasts in an effort to stave off motherhood. Some women relied on amulets; others held a pebble of jasper during coitus, or pressed to their left temple a cloth soaked in the oil of a barberry tree. These last methods may have succeeded in distracting them from experiencing orgasm; it was commonly held that enjoyment of sex would surely lead to conception.

More sophisticated methods were introduced from other cultures, especially from the Middle East. Women learned that it was possible to stuff their vaginas with a cloth or sponge, and some moistened the material with diluted lemon juice, an effective spermicide. A half lemon, squeezed dry, was tried as a cervical cap. Some worldly women insisted on *coitus interruptus*. The only sure way to avoid pregnancy, they convinced their lovers, was "to let no drop reach me." [6]

In general, contraception failed. Not only were most methods primitive, but the menstrual cycle was not yet understood. It was widely believed that conception would most likely occur during menstruation or immediately following, with a safe period coming at the midpoint of the cycle.

Even if Margaret had been able to bear more children, her own predilection toward asceticism made periods of celibacy likely even before she took her vow of chastity. Henry Stafford may have acceded to his wife's preferences. There were rumors that Margaret's marriage to Stanley was arranged with the stipulation that it not be consummated.[7]

Though her husbands may have offered her some companionship, it was not until 1494, when she was fifty-three, that she met the man with whom she could share an intimate friendship. Twenty-seven when he met Margaret in London, John Fisher was, until the end of her life, her confidant, counselor, and companion.

He was born in Beverly, the son of a mercer, Robert Fisher, who died when John was ten. At fourteen or fifteen, the youth entered Cambridge to prepare for ordination. He received his first degree in 1488, his master's in 1491, and in December of that year was ordained at York.

Just three years later he was chosen to be a university proctor. In 1497 he was master of Michaelhouse College at Cambridge and had succeeded Richard Fitzjames as Margaret's confessor. Fitzjames did not inspire in Margaret the same love and trust as Fisher did. He left Margaret's service when he became bishop of Rochester, the smallest and poorest diocese in England. The bishopric was commonly regarded as the first step up the episcopal ladder. Its revenues were a mere £300 per year, and even its ancient cathedral, begun by St. Augustine, the first archbishop of Canterbury, in 604, did not inspire its clergy to remain.

Fitzjames became bishop of Chichester, then of London, a more eminent and lucrative position. Fisher succeeded him at Rochester, promoted by Henry VII with the blessings of his mother. But it was not only Margaret's urging and prayers that won the post for the young minister. Richard Fox, then bishop of Winchester, also urged Henry to place Fisher at Rochester. "There are, perhaps, many who believe that his mother, the Countess of Richmond and Derby, that noble and incomparable lady, dear to me by so many titles, obtained the bishopric for me by her prayer to her son," Fisher wrote to Fox. "But the facts are entirely different, as your lordship knows well." [8]

Henry admitted that he decided on the appointment because he was impressed by Fisher's wisdom, virtue, and especially by the conduct of his life: "I know well it shulde corage many other to lyve vertuosely." [9]

For Fisher, Rochester was not a stopping place but a home. He stayed there, residing with "his flock" until his death. He was totally devoted to bringing the word of God to the common people. Earnest and serious in his work, he was, like Margaret, ascetic in his living. They felt an immediate kinship and a deep mutual respect.

In the fourteenth century, after the Black Plague, when the economy forced many off the land and out of work, common laborers and middle class alike resented the ostentatious living of men whose devotion should have been to higher values. The foremost opponent of the Church as it then existed was John Wycliffe, a Yorkshire-born, Oxford-educated priest, who, from his rectory at Lutterworth, issued books, pamphlets, and treatises — and the Gospels translated into the tongue of the people, English. Wycliffe held that the Bible, not the admonitions of priests, was the Church's real medium of instruction, and he urged his followers to read the Scriptures for themselves. As literacy spread, men and women found, for the first time, that the word of God was accessible to them and could be interpreted in many ways. They could be self-sufficient, independent of the authority of the clergy. "This lore that Christ taught us is enough for this life," said Wycliffe.

The clergy, as expected, found Wycliffe's teachings heretical. But another of Wycliffe's tenets won the support of some of the aristocracy, and that support enabled the radical theologian to continue his work. Wycliffe attacked the clergy for their accumulation of wealth and land, and such noblemen as John of Gaunt saw that attack as potentially beneficial to himself and his heirs. Church land, if confiscated, would revert to the original owners. Gaunt would stand to become even richer than he was if he could regain lost property. He supported Wycliffe, at least for a time, and buffeted the attacks of the clergy against him.

Wycliffe cut deeply into the entrenched rites of the Church. He attacked the Eucharist, claiming that the miracle of transubstantiation was not enacted at every mass, and believed that other sacraments were empty of meaning. He preached that there was another road to salvation: man must lead a good life. It was no wonder that throughout the last quarter of the fourteenth century and into the fifteenth, men and women who looked with sorrow on their turbulent world attached themselves to the teachings of Wycliffe. Called Lollards, their name derived from the French term for "babbling" and reflected the scorn that was heaped on the reformers from the first. Lollards were seen as heretics and were burned. The aristocracy, once the attack on Church lands failed, quickly moved away, and religious dissension became lodged only in the lower and middle classes. By the time Wycliffe died, in 1384, Lollardry had already become a formidable movement in England.

Many were fearful of Lollardry, both because it seemed antiorthodox and because it was a mass movement that threatened the values on which society had for so long been based. "Defend Us From All Lollardry," implored one poet.

> Lo, he that can be cristes clerc,
>> And knowe the knottes of his crede,
> Now may se a wonder werke,
>> Of harde happes to take goud heede.
> The dome of dethe is hevy drede
>> For hym that wol not mercy crie;
> Than is my rede, for muche ne mede,
>> That no man melle of Lollardrye . . .

> The game is nought to lolle so hie
>> Ther fete failen fondement;
> and yut is a moch folie
>> for fals beleve to ben brent.
>> ther the bibell is al myswent,
>>> To jangle of Job or Jeremye,
>> That construen hit after her entent
>>> for lewde lust of lollardie.

> Hit is unkyndly for a knight,
>> That shuld a kynges castel kepe,

To bable the bibel day & night
    In restyng tyme when he shuld slepe;
    & carefoly awey to crepe,
        for alle the chief of chivalrie.
    wel aught hym to waile & wepe,
        That suyche lust hath in lollardie . . .

I trowe ther be no knight alyve
    that wold have don so open a shame,
for that crafte to studi or strive,
    hit is no gentel mannes game;
    but if hym lust to have a name
        of pelour under ipocrasie,
    & that wer a foule defame
        to have suyche lose of lollardie . . .

and under colour of suiche lollynge,
    To shape sodeyn surreccion
Agaynst oure liege lord kynge,
    with fals ymaginacion.
    & for that corsed conclusion,
        by dome of knighthode & clergie,
Now turneth to confusion
    the cory sekte of lollardie.

For holy writ berith witnes,
    He that fals is to his kyng,
That shamful deth & hard distres.
    shal be his dome at his endynge.
    Than double deth for suyche lollynge
        is hevy, when we shul hennes hye.
    Now, lord, that madest of nought all thinge,
        defende us all fro lollardie.[10]

Margaret Beaufort and John Fisher attempted to counter Lollardry by efforts that employed similar tactics. Instead of Wycliffe's "poor priests," who would bring the Gospels to the people, Margaret amply endowed well-educated theologians who could resurrect the strength of the church for her son's subjects.

At the time she met Fisher, Margaret was interested in devoting her considerable wealth to God and the curing of souls rather than to the aggrandizement of the Church. Her interest had been in the Abbey of St. Peter at Westminster, but Fisher soon convinced her of the need for secular priests, rather than monks, to spread God's word among the people. She shifted her attentions and her endowments from the abbey to Cambridge, where she first founded two readerships in divinity.

The readers brought theology directly to laymen. They were elected every year by the chancellor and vice-chancellor of the university, and were all doctors, bachelors, or candidates for a degree in theology. For one hour each day they were commissioned to read to anyone, without fee, such works chosen by the school as uplifting and worthy. Each was paid just over £13 per year for his services. The salary was a grand one for the day, more than that of any minister in Cambridge and nearly as much as the whole yearly revenue of the Priory of St. Edmund. But it was Margaret's belief, and Fisher's, that such a service was indispensable. Sermons had fallen into disuse in the fifteenth century. Because of the fear of Lollardry, anyone who was not an ordained minister could be subjected to severe penalties for preaching, and the sermon itself took on a pejorative cast. In the countryside, clergy were supposed to preach to their congregations once every three months, but many did not fulfill even that minimum.

The readerships, therefore, were a way of providing direct communication from the Church to the people, under the sanction of the university. The ample remuneration would ensure that preachers of high quality and ability could be enlisted for the task.

Later, since she believed the readerships were a successful endeavor, Margaret established a preachership that paid £10 per year to the Lady Margaret Preachers. These men agreed to preach six sermons each year for three years, including one every second year in London and the rest in towns of Hertfordshire, Cambridgeshire, and Lincolnshire.

From 1505 on, Margaret was a frequent visitor to Cambridge, where private rooms, with a separate oratory overlooking a chapel, were set aside for her above the master's lodge of Christ's College. Christ's College itself owed its existence to Margaret. She had told Fisher that she wanted to found a new college at Cambridge, and he chose Godshouse, located opposite St. Andrew's Church, which had been founded during the reign of Henry VI. Originally a grammar school, it had grown into a college after a grant from Henry VI of two cottages, some outbuildings, and a garden. Though the king had planned to provide funds to maintain sixty scholars, the revenues were enough to support only a master and four fellows — hardly the community of scholars that Henry had envisioned.

With Margaret's help, the college was rebuilt and refunded. Now called Christ's College, it had an endowment large enough to maintain a master, twelve fellows, and forty-seven scholars. With her usual attention to details, Margaret provided also for a nurse to be engaged for the college, for special facilities in which patients could be housed in case of plague, and for the granting of visiting privileges to John Fisher for the duration of his life.

Margaret's business affairs were not limited to her endowments at Cambridge. As the holder of vast estates, she often was required to enter into contracts, bring suit for herself or her associates, invest her money in businesses, oversee the affairs of her wards. Two letters survive that deal specifically with land contracts, and Margaret showed herself, not surprisingly, to be firm and knowledgeable about her rights. In the first, she writes regarding a land dispute with the heirs of William Paston II. The letter, couched in polite prose, is no less than an ultimatum.

By the Kings Moder

Trusty and right welbeloved, we greet you well. And wher by the meanes of our trusty and right welbeloved Sir Reynold Bray, Sir Thomas Lovell and Sir Henry Heydon, knights, there was a full agreement made and concluded, and also put in writinge, betwen our trusty and right welbeloved Sir John Savile, knight, and Gilbert Talbot, esquier, on th'one partie, and yow on th'other, for divers lands which they ought to have in the right of their wives, daughters and heyers to William Paston, esquier, their late fader deceassed, which lands ye by mighty power kepe and witholde from them without any just title, as they afferme; and albeit the said agrement was made by your minde and consent, yet ye ne doe performe the same, to our merveile if it be so.

Wherefore we desier and also counsell yow without delay upon the sight hereof now shortly to ride to the court to the said arbitrators now ther being, with whom ye shall finde your adverse partie, or other in their names fully authorized, to abide such final ende and conclusion in the premisses as shall be consonant with the said agrement, without further troubles or busines therin herafter to be had; and that ye will thus do in any wise so as we be not driven through your defalte to put to our hands for further remedye to be had in the premisses.

Yeven under our signet at our mannor of Colly Weston the xth day of Februarye.[11]

The second, written later, is as forthright in its demands.

By the Kinges modre

Trusty and welveloved, we grete you wele, and pray you in our name to have the conynve of a bill herin closed in good and deliberate examinacion, and therupon to set such cude and ordinate direction as shalbe consonant to justice, right, and good conscience, so as for lakke therof the partie plaintief have no cause reasounable to pursue furthre unto us in that behalve, as we trust you.

Yeven undere our signet at our manour of Colyweston the xth day of Aprill.

Margaret R.[12]

Like many landowners, she believed that revenues could be collected, and estates run, most efficiently by a centralized staff. Only in Wales did she have difficulty managing the estates, despite the appointment of competent receivers. The Welsh estates were largely those which Margaret was managing for her ward, Edward Stafford, son of the slain duke of Buckingham. Margaret was meticulous in her handling of her ward's finances and would allow no funds to be wasted. Still, it was often impossible for debts to be collected, and she was forced to write off a deficit of over £2000 once she knew the money would never be forthcoming.

Though business affairs occupied much of her time, her real interest was in scholarship and the religious life. After Margaret's endowments to Cambridge became known in the academic world, she was entreated to take an interest in Oxford, by far the more prestigious of the two universities. But, though she set up one readership there, she was convinced by Fisher to devote her funds to his alma mater.

* * *

Margaret Beaufort and John Fisher shared a perception of history that resulted in a deep, untenable sorrow coloring every moment of their lives. Though Margaret's political scheming had been successful, she did not glory in that success and in the frivolities of the royal court. Instead, she felt constantly that her son's good fortune was precarious, as was her own, and that she must never pretend that the illusion of grandeur was, indeed, reality. Fisher admitted that he wanted to set an example in "humility, sobriety and contempt of the world," which well describes the intent of Margaret's life, as well. Both were highly self-disciplined, in reaction to a world that was lawless, morally chaotic, and politically decadent. The sins they both tried continually to expiate were not only the inherent moral sins of every human being; they were also the sins of their fathers, brothers, cousins — of all around them. Only by living an exemplary life could each justify his own existence.

"Whiles thou are in this life, and whiles thou hast time and space," Fisher said in one of his sermons, "study to make amends for thy sins. Study to store thy soul by true contrition and sorrow for thy sins. Study here to wash the same often with the gracious water of tears. Study to cleanse thy soul with often renewing confession. Study here by thy good and gracious works to pay thy own debts before thy departure hence."

Fisher knew the creed of Margaret's life. Always, she tried to respond to a world that seemed bereft of virtue.

> Virtues & good lyving is cleped [called] ypocrisie;
> trowthe & godis law is cleped heresie . . .
> trewe prechinge & penaunce is cleped folie.
> pride is cleped honeste,
> and coveityse wisdom.
> richesse is cleped worthynes,
> and lecherie kyndely thing,
> robberie good wynnynge,
> & glotenye but murthe.
> envye and wrathe men clepen rightfulness;
> slouthe men clepen nedfulnes
> to norshe mennes kynde.
> and thus mannes lif that shulde be holi
> is turned into cursednes.
> rightwisdom is not dred,
> and mercy is but scorned . . .[13]

The violence of the time was odious to both Margaret and John Fisher. They believed that if religion were brought closer to the lives of the commoners, the turbulent atmosphere might be counteracted. Both knew that criminal law was often ignored, and perpetrators of violent crimes were sought after as desirable mercenaries. The continuing wars had made arms more easily available and men more ready to resort to their use. If Margaret's insistence on leading an exemplary life seems too rigorous, it is necessary only to look at the world she experienced and the alternative she saw as inevitable. Vigilance, she had learned early, was imperative. But one had to look not only over one's shoulder, but inside the soul.

* * *

No one was more aware of the seeds of violence than Henry VII. Like Margaret, he believed that livery and maintenance were evil forces that must be obliterated. He took a hard stand against the practices, effecting changes that Henry VI could not and Edward IV would not make. Heavy fines were incurred by any nobleman who paraded his retainers. Informers were encouraged, and offenders were summoned to the king's Star Chamber to be judged by the chancellor, treasurer, keeper of the privy seal, one bishop, one temporal peer, and two chief judges. Gradually the practices ceased.

Henry could not, however, avoid political threats. In 1491 another pretender to the throne appeared in Ireland. But this young man was taken more seriously than the hapless Simnel. Seventeen-year-old Perkin Warbeck claimed to be Richard, duke of York, the younger son of Edward IV, escaped from the Tower to claim the crown as Richard IV.

For eight years he was to vex Henry as he gained support first from Margaret of Burgundy, the sister of Edward IV, and then from James IV of Scotland. Unlike Simnel, Warbeck was bold in his assertion of birthright and communicated directly with foreign monarchs for their alliance. In September 1493 he wrote to Isabella of Castile, outlining his biography and calling Henry VII a usurper of the throne that was rightfully his. In July 1497 he issued a proclamation that claimed Henry had "by subtle false means" obtained the crown. He called Henry "our extreme, and mortal enemy," who would try to destroy Warbeck by conspiracy with the nobles. He attacked Henry's financial policy: "Our said Enemy not regarding the wealth and prosperity of this land, but only the safeguard and surety of his person hath . . . caused to be conveyed from thence to other places the treasure of this our realm, purposing to depart after in proper person with many other Estates of the Land, being now at his rule and disposition." [14] Warbeck's purpose was to rally support among the English, but he eventually failed.

By 1493 Henry had identified the imposter, and within two years had issued attainders against those who he believed supported him. The delay in issuing the attainders may have been caused by the shocking identity of one of the alleged traitors. Sir William Stanley, the king's uncle, was foremost among those arrested and tried in January 1495. Henry's loyalty to his stepfather's brother was destroyed by the facts before him. He was convinced of Stanley's treachery, as were others who sat in judgment, and Stanley was ordered to be hanged, drawn, and quartered. Later, the sentence was commuted to the more lenient beheading, which was enacted on February 16.

Stanley's actions did not alter the relationship Henry enjoyed with his stepfather, nor did it diminish Thomas Stanley's standing in the court. Whatever his private feelings, Thomas Stanley apparently remained firmly behind his stepson and his own wife. Margaret, for her part, had seen dissension between brothers explode into political disasters during other reigns. She was not so much shocked as saddened that her son would have to suffer another's treachery.

Stanley's death frightened any other Englishmen who might have planned to join Warbeck's plot, but Henry still had to contend with Yorkist supporters in Scotland and on the continent. Only through diplomacy did Henry manage to achieve a truce with James IV, and Margaret of Burgundy's aid to the pretender was not sufficient to cause an insurrection. By the end of September 1497, Warbeck surrendered and confessed. Henry did not immediately punish the young man who had caused so much turmoil. But neither did he set him free. Warbeck balked at being a house prisoner. In June 1498 he escaped, was recaptured, and set in stocks for half a day. Then he was transferred to a scaffold, where he stood displayed from ten one morning to three in the afternoon, "excedyngly wondred upon." [15] But the punishment did not deter him from attempting yet another escape. At the end of the month he jumped from a window and was found the next day seven miles away, hiding in a monastery. Henry could do nothing but arrest him and, in 1499, have him hanged.

John Skelton, the court's poet laureate, penned a satire about Warbeck.

> Of all nacyons under the hevyn,
> These frantyke foolys I hate most of all;
> In pevyshnes yet they snapper and fall,
> Which men the viii dedly syn call.
> This punysh proud, thys prendergest [pretender],
> When he is well, yet can he not rest.

"Lo, Jak wold be a jentylman!" scoffed Skelton. "Too fat is hys fantsy, hys wyt is too lene." [16]

Warbeck's threat was no fantasy to Henry, who was ever aware of the existence of Yorkist supporters in England, Burgundy, and France. Rumors reached him constantly, and as early as 1487 he issued a proclamation against the spreading of false news.

> Forasmuch as many of the King our sovereign lord's subjects be disposed daily to hear feigned, contrived, and forged tidings and tales; and the same tidings and tales, neither dreading God nor his highness, utter and tell again as though they were true, to the great hurt of divers of his subjects and to his grievous displeasure . . .
>
> The King our sovereign lord straightly chargeth and commandeth that no manner person . . . utter nor tell any such tidings or tales . . . upon pain to be set on the pillory, there to stand as long as it shall be thought convenient to the mayor, bailiff, or other officer.[17]

The King's Bench was made of marble; but, as Henry knew too well, it was a fragile seat.

XI

The House of Mourning

The heart of the wise is in the house of mourning;
but the heart of fools is in the house of mirth.
ECCLESIASTES 7:4

BY 1496 Henry and Elizabeth had had four children. Three years after Arthur, in 1489, Margaret, named for her grandmother, was born. At fourteen she would be married to James IV of Scotland in a futile attempt to join England in friendship with her northern neighbor. A second son, Henry, was born at Greenwich on June 28, 1491. Another daughter, Mary, followed in March of 1496. In 1499 Edmund was born, named for the king's father; he lived only into the spring of 1500.

The hopes of the Tudors were vested in Arthur. At his birth, Bernard André composed one hundred poems in celebration. Later, the Oxford-educated André served as Arthur's tutor, to be followed by such eminent scholars as Thomas Linacre, the physician and classicist who had studied in Rome and Florence. By the time Arthur was fifteen, besides having studied Latin grammar, he had read some of Homer, Virgil, Ovid, Terence, Cicero, Thucydides, Caesar, Livy, and Tacitus. He was created prince of Wales on November 29, 1489, and as heir to the throne inspired many rumors about his marriage prospects.

If the Tudor family was to survive and retain the crown, as both Margaret Beaufort and her son intensely desired, marriage alliances must be farsighted and careful. Of all such bonds the king hoped to realize for England, that with Spain was most important. Henry followed his predecessors in believing that only if France were surrounded by England's allies would the threat of war ever be diminished. England's negotiations with Ferdinand of Aragon and his wife, Isabella of Castile, were to culminate in the marriage of Arthur with their daughter, Catherine of Aragon.

In May 1501, Catherine left her homeland and the domination of her parents to become princess of Wales. To welcome the young princess, Henry, as his letter to John Paston III indicates, commissioned squires throughout the country to turn out:

By the Kinge

Trusty and welbeloved, we grete yow well, letting yow wete that our derest cousins the Kinge and Queene of Spaine have signified unto us by their sundry letters that the right excellent Princesse, the Lady Katherine ther daughter, shalbe transported from the parties of Spaine aforesaid to this our Realme about the moneth of May next comeinge for the solemnpnization of matrimoney betweene our deerest sonne the Prince and the said Princesse. Wherfore we, consideringe that it is right fittinge and necessarye, aswell for the honour of us as for the lawde and praise of our said Realme, to have the said Princesse honourable received at her arriveall, have appointed you to be amonge others to yeve attendance for the receivinge of the said Princesse; willinge and desiringe yow to prepare your-selfe for that intent, and so to continue in a redynesse upon an houres warninge, till that by our other letters we shall advertise yow of the day and time of her arrivall and where ye shall yeve your said attendance; and not to fayle therein as ye tender our pleasure, the honour of your-selfe, and of this our foresaid Realme.[1]

After a turbulent trip across the sea, the fifteen-year-old princess, who could speak no English and no French, arrived with her attendants at Plymouth, on October 2, 1501. Racked with seasickness and weak after her voyage, she remained at the coast for a month, while gaping Englishmen crowded to see the strangely dressed Spaniards and staged gala festivities in their honor. Not until November 12 did she ride, escorted by royalty, into London for the wedding celebration. The chronicler Hall tantalized his readers with his description of the pageantry.

And because I will not be tedious to you, I passe over the wyse devises, the prudent speches, the costly woorkes, the conninge portratures practised and set foorth in vii goodly beautiful pageauntes erected & set up in diverse places of the citie. I leave also ye goodly ballades, ye swete armony, the Musicall instrumentes, which sounded with heavenly noyes on every side of the strete. I omit farther, the costly apparel both of goldsmythes woorke and embraudery, the ryche jewelles, the massy cheynes, the sturynge horsses, the beautifull bardes and the glitteryng trappers, both with belles and spangles of golde. I pretermit also the ryche apparell of the pryncesse, the straunge fashion of the Spanyshe nacion, the beautie of the Englishe ladyes, the goodly demeanure of the young damosels, the amorous countenaunce of the lusty bachelers. I passe over also the fyne engrayned clothes, the costly furres of the citezens, standynge on skaffoldes, rayed from Gracechurche to Paules. What should I speke of the oderiferous skarlettes, the fyne velvet, the pleasaunt furres, the massye chaynes, which the Mayre of London with the senate, sitting on horsebacke at the little conduyte in Chepe, ware on their bodyes, & about their neckes. I will not molest you with rehersyng the ruche arras, the costly tapestry, the fyne clothes both of golde & silver, the curious velvettes, the beautiful sattens, nor the pleasaunte sylkes, which did hange in every strete where she passed, the wyne that ranne continually out of the conduytes, the graveling and rayling of the stretes nedeth not to be remembered.[2]

The bride was a plump adolescent with waist-long auburn hair. At her wedding she wore a white mantilla bordered with gold, pearls, and precious stones. Her gown fanned out from the waist in tiers of hoops, and its sleeves were large and draped. The fair-haired Arthur, considerably slimmer than his wife, also wore white: coat, breeches, hose, and shirt of white satin.

As was the custom, Henry, Elizabeth, and Margaret Beaufort watched the wedding ceremonies from behind a specially constructed latticed box so that the honored pair could bask in unadulterated admiration.

"Every day endeth, and night ensueth," Hall reminds us, but what happened on the wedding night was, later, open to much conjecture. Hall left no doubt as to how the night was spent. "This lusty prince and his beautifull bryde were brought and joyned together in one bed naked, and there did that acte whiche to the performaunce & full consummacion of matrimony was moost requysite and expedient." The next morning, Arthur summoned his servants and asked for water, claiming an unquenchable thirst. "At which thinge one of hys chambrelaynes mervallynge, required the cause of his drouth. To whome he answered merely saiyng, I have thys nyght bene in the middest of Spayne, whiche is a hote region, & that journey maketh me so drye, and if thou haddest bene under that hote clymate, thou wouldest have bene dryer then I." [3]

Arthur and Catherine set up their court at Ludlow, where the prince of Wales reigned. Soon Arthur became ill, perhaps from plague, perhaps from a new outbreak of the puzzling sweating-sickness. Five months after his wedding, he was dead. Henry was grief-stricken, but his first duty was to his mourning wife, who nearly collapsed at the news. After he comforted her, he too succumbed to profound sorrow. Elizabeth would not leave his side; she told him that he must think of England and of her, and not allow himself to be undone by the tragedy. "And," she added, "remember that my lady, your mother, had never no more children but you only, yet God, by his grace, has ever preserved you and brought you where you are now. Over and above, God has left you yet a fair prince and two fair princesses; and God is still where he was, and we are both young enough . . ." [4]

God was still in his heaven, but Elizabeth was thirty-six. On February 11, 1503, she gave birth to a daughter, Katherine. Just a month before, William Parron, the court astrologer, had predicted that Elizabeth would live to be eighty. She died within days of her daughter's birth. To her adoring subjects, the death of the young queen was a great loss.

> O ye that put your trust and confidence,
> In worldly joy and frayle prosperitie,
> That so lyve here as ye should never hence,
> Remember death and loke her uppon me.
> Ensaumple I thynke there may no better be.
> Your self wotte well that in this realme was I,
> Your quene but late, and lo now here I lye.
>
> Was I not borne of old worthy linage?
> Was not my mother queene my father kynge?
> Was I not a kinges fere [wife] in marriage?
> Had I not plenty of every pleasaunt thyng?
> Mercifull god this is a straunge reckenyng.
> Rychesse, honour, welth, and auncestry
> Hath me forsaken and lo now here I ly.

Yet was I late promised otherwyse,
This yere to live in welth and delice.
Lo whereth commeth thy blandishyng promyse,
Of false astrolagy and devynatrice,
Of goddes secretes makyng thy self so wyse.
How true is for this yere thy prophecy.
The yere is lasteth, and lo now here I ly.

Where are our Castels, now where are our Towers,
Goodly Rychmonde sone art thou gone from me,
At Westminster that costly worke of yours,
Myne owne dere lorde, now shall I never see.
Almighty god vouchesafe to graunt that ye,
For you and your children well may edefy.
My palace bylded is, and lo now here I ly.

Adew my owne dere spouse, my worthy lorde,
The faithfull love that dyd us both combyne,
In marriage and peasable concorde,
Into your handes here I cleane resyne,
To be bestowed uppon your children and myne.
Erst we you father, & now must ye supply,
The mothers part also, for lo now here I ly.

Farewell my doughter lady Margarete,
God wotte full oft it greved hath my mynde,
That ye should go where we should seldome mete [Scotland]
Now am I gone, and have left you behynde.
O mortall folke that we be very blynde.
That we least feare, full oft it is most nye,
From you depart I fyrst, and lo now here I lye.

Farewell Madame my lordes worthy mother,
Comfort your sonne, and be ye of good chere.
Take all a worth, for it will be no nother.
Farewell my doughter Katherine [of Aragon] late the fere,
To prince Arthur myne owne chylde so dere
It booteth not for me to wepe or cry,
Pray for my soule, for lo now here I ly.

Adew lord Henry my loving sonne adew.
Oure lorde encrease your honour and estate,
Adew my doughter Mary bright of hew.
God make you vertuous, wyse and fortunate.

Adew swete hart my litle doughter Kate,
Thou shalt swete babe such is thy desteny
Thy mother never know, for lo now here I ly.

Lady Cicyly, Anne and Katheryne.
Farewell my welbeloved sisters three,
O lady Briget other sister myne,
Lo here the end of worldly vanitee.
Now well are ye that earthly foly flee,
And hevenly thynges love and magnify,
Farewell and pray for me, for lo now here I ly.

Adew my lordes, adew my ladies all,
Adew my faithfull servauntes every chone,
Adew my commons whom I never shall
See in this world, wherfore to the alone,
Immortall god verely three and one,
I me commende, thy infinite mercy,
Shew to thy servant, for lo now here I ly.[5]

The queen's body was buried in Henry's newly constructed chapel at Westminster.

Now, for the second time, Margaret Beaufort assumed the role of mother. But instead of caring for a single son, a boy only she believed would be king, she took on the nurturing of the king's family, the recognized heirs to the Tudor throne. She doted especially on her only surviving grandson, Henry. At twelve Henry was still a frail youth, just gaining strength after a sickly childhood. He was never alone — watched over carefully, since on him alone the kingship descended. He could leave his rooms only to sport in an enclosed park, and even then he was closely guarded. He was instructed not to speak in public, except to his father, and to allow no one to speak to him. Though he was now prince of Wales, he was not sent to Ludlow to carry on Arthur's duties, probably for fear that he too would succumb to illness.

Yet within the confines of the palace at Richmond, he managed to develop into an athletic youth, excelling at tilting, riding, archery, tennis. He showed exceptional talent for music, learning to play lute, virginal, and organ. He could sing well, sight-reading the popular songs of the day, often accompanied by one of his courtiers. He composed several instrumental pieces, songs, and rounds.

Margaret engaged as one of his tutors John Skelton, the poet laureate and a cleric, whose cynical and often lewd verses were unknown to the pious Margaret. She was aware only of his court verses, such as his homage to the king in 1488, at the feast of St. George.

> O moste famous noble king! thy fame doth spring and spreade,
> Henry the Seventh, our soverain, in eiche regeon;
> All England hath cause thy grace to love and dread,
> Seing embassadores secke fore protectyon,
> For ayd, helpe, and succore, which lyeth in thie electyone.
> England, now rejoyce, for joyous mayest thou bee,
> To see thy kyng so floreshe in dignetye.
>
> This realme a seasone stoode in greate jupardie,
> When that noble prince deceased, King Edward,
> Which in his dayes gate honore full nobly;
> After his decesse mighe hand all was marr'd;
> Eich regione this land dispised, mischefe when they hard:
> Wherefore rejoyse, for joyous mayst thou be,
> To see thy kynge so floresh in high degnetye . . .
>
> O knightly ordere, clothed in robes with gartere!
> The queen's grace and thy mother clothed in the same;
> The nobles of thie realme riche in araye, aftere,
> Lords, knights, ladyes, unto thy great fame:
> Now shall all embassadors know thie noble name,
> By thy feaste royal; nowe joyeous mayst thou be;
> To see thie king so florishinge in dignetye . . .[6]

Skelton was a prolific poet, whose inspiration could come even from his assignment to the prince of Wales.

> The honour of Englond I learnyd to spelle,
> In dygnyte royalle that doth excelle:
> Note and marke wyl thys parcele;
> I gave hym drynke of the sugryd welle
> Of Eliconys waters crystallyne,
> Aqueintyng hym with the Musys nyne.
> Yt commyth the wele me to remorde,
> That creaunset was to thy sofre[yne] lorde:
> It plesyth that noble prince royalle
> Me as hys master for to call
> In hys lernyng primordialle.[7]

Besides overseeing her grandchildren, Margaret was concerned with the fate of the lonely widowed Catherine, whose welfare depended on her father and father-in-law, both of whom saw her as a pawn in their diplomatic game. Naturally, Margaret hoped that her son would succeed in keeping Catherine in England to marry the new prince of Wales, Henry. The Spanish princess was too important for England's international influence, and for the Tudor dynasty, to allow her to be returned to Spain, as her father at first insisted.

Ferdinand, whose own wife had recently died, wanted his daughter returned and refused to pay any more of her dowry to her late husband's family. Catherine, for her part — though her part was little considered — objected to marrying a twelve-year-old child and wished to go home.

Though Margaret Beaufort and her husband had entertained Spanish diplomats before and after Catherine's marriage to Arthur, she could hardly communicate with the young woman and knew little of her. She had once advised Catherine, by letter, that she would do well to learn French so that she could better assimilate herself into the English nobility, but apparently Catherine did not take her advice at the time. Though Margaret was sympathetic to Catherine's plight, there was little she could do to ease the unhappiness the young woman felt.

Catherine's letters to her father bared her pain at being forced to live in what she described as near-poverty and at being ignored in all her requests. She reminded her father that, as his daughter, she could do nothing but rely on his mercy. She was in debt not for jewels, plate, or frivolities, but for food for herself and her servants. She explained to Ferdinand that she had gone to Henry in tears but that he had replied that he was not responsible for her. She was growing thin, she said, and her health was deteriorating.

She described herself as if she were a prisoner, with no rights and no means of asserting her will, at the mercy of her keepers. She begged her father to send an ambassador with high authority and rank, "because he has more to do than your highness thinks, or I could tell you." [8] She doubted that her father truly understood what she suffered, and hoped that an ambassador would report the truth and be believed. "I believe your highness would be frightened at that which I have passed through," she wrote.

One explanation for Henry's strange coolness toward his daughter-in-law, and his mother's lack of intervention on Catherine's behalf, was the young woman's apparently indiscreet relationship with a friar who had been sent to her from Spain. One emissary reported to Ferdinand that Catherine was "so submissive to a friar whom she has as confessor, that he makes her do a great many things which very much grieved the King." The incident involved a request that Catherine go to Richmond with the king and his family. Catherine at first agreed, but the friar allegedly instructed her not to go. The princess argued meekly; the friar insisted that she stay. Finally Catherine sent a message to Henry's daughter Mary that she would not be able to go to Richmond because of illness. All around her were convinced that she was well and was acting only on the instructions of her confessor.

"These and other things of a thousand times worse kind the friar makes her do . . ." continued the emissary. "May God forgive me, but now that I know so well the affairs of the Princess's household, I acquit the King of England of a great and very great portion of the blame which I hitherto gave to him, and I do not wonder at what he has done, but at that which he does not do, especially as he is of such a temperament as to wish that in house and kingdom that be done without contradiction which he desires and orders." [9]

In another letter, the emissary, Membrilla, added, "I wrote to your Lordship about a friar who is here as confessor to the Princess, who would to God he were in his monastery, and not here, because he neither brings nor has brought any good, and if he is here much longer he will bring greater injury upon her Highness . . ." Membrilla urged Ferdinand to withdraw the friar, claiming that the English were becoming increasingly angered by his continued presence in their country. "May God destroy me," he implored, "if I see in the friar anything for which she should have so much affection, for he has neither learning, nor appearance, nor manners, nor competency, nor credit, and yet if he wishes to preach a new law they have to believe it." [10]

Catherine was well aware of Membrilla's feelings, and his letter to Ferdinand accompanied her own, in which she urged her father not to believe his ambassador. "If he writes anything about my household and especially about my confessor," she wrote, "your Highness will not credit it. For by my salvation, and by the life of your Highness, he does not tell the truth if he states anything except that [the confessor] serves me well and loyally . . . I shall not believe that your

Highness looks upon me as your daughter if you do not punish it, and order the ambassador to confine himself to the affairs of his embassy, and to abstain from meddling in the affairs of my household." [11]

The frightened adolescent who had come to England only a few years before had become a woman whose needs could not be set aside, yet she was always being manipulated. De Puebla, another Spanish representative who proved a great disappointment to Catherine, was much in favor of her marriage with Henry. He reported to Ferdinand, "There is no finer youth in the world than the Prince of Wales. He is already taller than his father, and his limbs are of a gigantic size. He is as prudent as is to be expected from a son of Henry VII.

"The Princess of Wales is well," he continued, "and her health constantly improves. She suffers from no other evil than the anxiety she feels because she has heard that her marriage is not yet rendered indissoluble." [12]

Finally Ferdinand agreed to the marriage, and Catherine herself was relieved that at least her penury would be alleviated. "It is impossible for me any longer to endure what I have gone through," she wrote to her father. She had sold her household goods to pay for necessities; she had suffered a particularly humiliating encounter with Henry, during which he informed her that he was not at all obligated to provide food for her and her servants, but would continue to do so out of the love he still bore her. "From this," Catherine wrote, "your Highness will see to what a state I am reduced, when I am warned that even my food is given to me almost as alms." [13]

The date of the marriage was not fixed — the couple would not marry until 1510 — and Catherine, waiting, was still treated as an outcast. "May your Highness give me satisfaction before I die," she pleaded with her father, "for I fear my life will be short, owing to my troubles." [14] She did not die, of course, nor were her troubles ended. In the next years, Henry VII grew ill, and, though he was only fifty, he felt himself to be an old man. Gout may have been complicated by consumption; his health deteriorated rapidly.

On April 21, 1509, the king died at Sheen. Margaret's intense grief sent her into isolated prayer, with only Bishop Fisher to offer consolation. Fisher's funeral sermon, delivered on May 9, offered in public the same consolation he had given to Margaret in the first hours of her son's death. "The Court of King Edward, the court of King Richard, and the court of the king that now is dead, where be they now? All they were but counterfeit images and disguising for a time, it was but play for a time. But the court of heaven is alway stable in one point where the officers change never. There is the true nobleness, the sure honour, the very glory." [15]

When Henry died, a great part of Margaret Beaufort died. She watched his body laid in a black velvet-lined coffin, marked by a white satin cross from end to end. She watched as the body was transported to Westminster Abbey and laid in the vault Henry had commissioned. She heard the heavy doors shut and saw the king's heralds strip off their tabards, hang them on the rails of the hearse, and exclaim in French, "The noble King Henry VII is dead!" Then they put on their tabards, and their cry resounded in Margaret's ears: "Vive le noble Roy Henry VIII!"

For the sixth time, Margaret witnessed the rise of a new king in England. This king, like the last, was of her own blood, a Tudor. She had seen him born and had watched over him as he grew into a tall, broad-shouldered, strong youth. But she did not feel the deep affinity with her grandson that she had with her son. This young king seemed to grow apart from her as he grew up. He was completely unlike the quiet, well-mannered, docile Arthur. He seemed to have inherited little from his father, a man all admitted was "sobre, moderate, honest, affable, courteous," and temperate in all things. At times she was in awe of the young Henry, at times frustrated by her inability to bring him close to her.

The king lived, but it was not the king to whom she could give her whole heart. Her great love, her only joy, was gone. She turned obsessively to religion, hardly appearing in public except at the coronation of Henry VIII.

XII

The Legacy

DESPITE THE PAIN of arthritis and the fatigue of illness, Margaret Beaufort devoted her final years entirely to religious causes. She was informed that in a certain convent the prioress and nuns were incontinent and living a dissolute life. She had them expelled, and converted the convent into a college for one master and six fellows, with however many scholars could be accommodated at any one time. The scholars were to be instructed in grammar and were required to pray daily for the king, his family, his ancestors, and his heirs.

The founding of such chantries was common among the nobility, who, for the price of an endowment, could have their souls prayed for eternally: effusive prayer was believed to shorten one's time in purgatory. Among Margaret's founded chantries were those at Collegiate Church in Wymbourn, in Salisbury, and at the University of Cambridge.

Margaret's concern for her mortality extended beyond the chantries to the making of her will, in June 1508. She provided that more than £133 be distributed among the poor, that £200 be set aside for funeral clothes, that her twelve poor men and women at Hatfield be maintained at her cost for the rest of their lives, that her servants be fairly rewarded, and, most important to her, that a new college be founded at Cambridge, to be called St. John's. The college would be established by the conversion of the Hospital of St. John, a task that Margaret assigned to John Fisher. "Forsooth . . . it was sore laborious and painful unto me that many times I was right sorry that ever I took that business upon me," Fisher wrote fourteen years later.

Besides the arduous task, Margaret left Fisher a pair of gilt pots, engraved with marguerites and the Beaufort portcullis, and a small cellar of gold, decorated with a chevron design and encrusted with pearls and a sapphire. Her aides were bequeathed various items of furnishings; one was given a volume of poetry by John Gower; another, a cup of gold.

To her son, alive when the will was written, she left five "of my best cuppes of gold with their covers" [1] and four books: a French book that began with the Book of Genesis and included "diverse stories," the second volume of Froissart's chronicles, a volume by one John Bokas, and "a grette volume of velom of the siege of Troye yn Englissh." [2] Her granddaughter Mary was to be given a girdle of gold with twenty-nine links and a large pomander at the end.

To her grandson Henry, she knew she was leaving the most precious and at the same time most onerous bequest: the kingdom of England. In June 1509, when she knew she was dying, Margaret called Henry to her bedside and begged him to accede to her last request. She urged him to obey John Fisher in all things, to heed his counsel and depend on his wisdom, to remember, too, her own teachings and the example of his father in conducting himself as king. She exhorted him to treat with reverence the Tudor legacy. Perhaps, when she died on June 29, 1509, she believed his hasty promises.

Henry VIII, now in early manhood, was as unlike his grandmother and father as anyone could be. "In the eighth Henry such beauty of mind and body is combined as to surprise and astonish," wrote Ludovico Falieri, the Venetian ambassador. "Grand stature, suited to his exalted position, showing the superiority of mind and character; a face like an angel's so fair it is ... He is accomplished in every manly exercise, sits his horse well, tilts with his lance, throws the quoit, shoots with his bow excellent well; he is a fine tennis player, and he practises all these gifts with the greatest industry ... He has been a student from his childhood; he knows literature, philosophy, and theology; speaks and writes Spanish, French, and Italian, besides Latin and English ..." [3] Henry was grand in stature and flamboyant in dress. In imitation of the king of France, he decided to let his beard grow, and the shimmering red-gold whiskers gave him a special distinction in his land of clean-shaven men.

He soon grew impatient with the righteous, virtuous, diligent Bishop Fisher. Instead, he took as his aide and confidant his father's chaplain, Thomas Wolsey. First bishop of Lincoln, Wolsey became archbishop of York, then abbot of St. Albans. Unlike Fisher, he coveted not only power but wealth. The king became closely allied with another prelate, James Stanley, Margaret's stepson and bishop of Ely. Despite his kinship with Margaret, James Stanley contradicted all that his stepmother had believed in.

Stanley had been a poor scholar from boyhood, much to the dismay of his father and stepmother. Still, plans were made to train him for the clergy — if only he could become minimally literate. He was incorrigibly lazy, however, and no progress was made in his education in England. The family decided to send him to Paris, where he was instructed to seek out Erasmus and become his pupil. No doubt his parents believed that some inspiration from the famous scholar might spur the mind of the indolent James. But Erasmus refused to teach him, convinced that he could never bring credit to his master's name, and James returned to England older but otherwise unchanged.

Through his stepmother's ecclesiastical influence, he was ordained and eventually promoted to the see of Ely. Bishop Morton's seat was thereby stained by the infamous James Stanley, whose licentious behavior scandalized the town and its environs even as far as London.

As the foremost executor of Margaret's will, John Fisher was forced to confront both Wolsey and Stanley when he attempted to establish St. John's College. Henry VIII's representative, Wolsey, was opposed to the establishment of the college because it diverted funds from the king's future inheritance. Stanley, like Wolsey, had no sympathy for the projected conversion of the Hospital of St. John, located within Ely and therefore under his jurisdiction. For no reason other than subbornness, Stanley refused to allow the hospital to be touched.

Though it would seem that the executors of Margaret's will might have exerted a certain strength and influence, not all were actively involved in their legal duties. Thomas Lovell, a man in high favor with the king, was a busy politician whose interest was in issues he considered much grander and potentially more lucrative. In addition, he was executor of the will of Henry VII, to his mind a weightier responsibility. Richard Fox, though he was a friend of Fisher's, was also a close friend of Wolsey's. He too had been educated at Oxford, as had most of the influential men of the period, and his sympathies lay there. Hugh Ashton, though he later became more active in Cambridge, was not a prime mover in the execution of Margaret's will. Only Henry Hornby was a strong supporter of Margaret's plan, and his influence was much below that of John Fisher's.

In all ways, Fisher stood alone. Many believed he faced the impossible, but for seven years he did not give up hope of realizing Margaret's dream. At first he won a great triumph when a papal bull was obtained that dissolved the hospital. This usurpation of Stanley's power was seen as a moral victory, and Fisher believed his task could proceed. But Wolsey, in the name of the king, still mightily opposed Fisher's efforts. The executors were forced to prove the will at the Court of Chancery and the Court of Arches. Initially they won their right to proceed with the execution of the will, yet Wolsey persisted, and it was clear to Fisher that a second suit would be lost. He abandoned his claim to the hospital, but not his determination to establish a college in Margaret's name.

Though no one knew then where the money came from, he somehow found revenues and appropriated three religious houses — the Hospital of Ospringe in Kent, the nunnery of Higham, with its three dissolute nuns, and the nunnery of Bromehall. In 1516 St. John's College opened. In his preamble to the statutes, Fisher finally revealed his source of funds: "The noble princess, Lady Margaret, Countess of Richmond, the foundress of this college, in her great condescension had a great desire to procure me a richer bishopric. But when she saw that her approaching death would frustrate this desire, she left me no small sum of money to use for my own purposes, which I mention lest anyone think that I have made this large endowment with other people's money." [4]

A portrait of Margaret Beaufort was hung in the college. She wears black, like the habit of a nun, with a wimple of white linen over her chin and neck. With her hands in prayer, she kneels before a desk on which lies an open book resting on a scarf of cloth of gold. A canopy of cloth of gold, with a red rose in the center, extends over her head. The arms of France and England appear at the back, with a ducal coronet flanked by an eagle on one side, a tiger on the other, and the Beaufort portcullis beneath.

Later, when Fisher was declared a founder of the college, he replied that he had acted only as Lady Margaret's servant, that he was only fulfilling his duty. She, for her part, had hoped that the youth who passed through the college would then go out and spread the word of God throughout England "with abundant fruit."

The statutes for the college were almost identical with those that Margaret had approved for Christ's College. Theology was of foremost importance, but the humanities were sanctioned: the scholars must not "turn aside to any Faculty other than Philosophy [which included the arts] and Theology." [5] The students must devote themselves to "the worship of God, the increase of the faith, and probity of morals." [6] They were expected to be serious and diligent. They could not have dogs or fly falcons for sport; they could play at dice or cards only during Christmas and only if they were fellows, not lowerclassmen. Hunting and hawking could be indulged in, but only outside the confines of the university.

Fisher was concerned that St. John's did not have the continuing interest of a rich benefactor, as had Christ's College. Because the school sorely needed appointments and books, he donated his own considerable library and the hangings, furnishings, and even the plate and drinking vessels from his apartments. These were legally owned by the college during Fisher's lifetime, but by a special indenture Fisher was given use of his belongings during the remainder of his life.

Fisher lived continuously with the memory of Margaret Beaufort. One month after her death, Fisher offered the traditional "mornynge remembraunce," which attests to his love for her and to her singular personality.

> She was bounteous & lyberall to every persone of her knowledge or aquayntaunce. Averyce and covetyse she moost hated. And sorowed it ful moche in al persones, But especyally in ony that belonged unto her. She was also of singular easynes to be spoken unto, & full curtayse answere she wolde make to all that came unto her. Of mervayllous gentylnesse she was unto all folkes, but specyally unto her owne, whom she trusted and loved ryghte tenderly. Unkynde she wolde not be unto no creature, ne forgetefull of ony kyndes or servyce done to her before, whiche is no lytel parte of veray noblenes. She was not vengeable, ne cruell, but redy a none to forgete and to forgyve injuries done unto her at the leest desyre or mocyon made unto her for the same. Mercyfull also & pyteous she was unto suche as was grevyd & wrongfully troubled And to them that were in puverty or sekenes or ony other myserye.[7]

Margaret Beaufort's wonderful gentleness, her piety, her kindness were not inherited by her grandson. Henry had grown corpulent in the first twenty years of his reign, and his ego seemed to burgeon proportionately. He styled himself "His Majesty," as did the emperors of Europe, and in foreign and domestic policy was impetuous and imperious. Fisher, with his unflagging sense of righteousness, was bound to conflict with his king's self-styled morality.

After some five years of marriage, Henry became bored with his twenty-nine-year-old wife and took his first lover, Elizabeth Bloundt, a lady in waiting to Catherine. The liaison lasted at least five years.

Elizabeth was not to keep her lover's affections. In 1521, Henry became enamoured of Mary Boleyn, recently married to William Carey, and the daughter of one of Henry's counselors. Mary did not allow her husband to stand in the way of her relationship with the king, nor did Carey presume to interfere. This affair also seems to have lasted some five years. By then, Henry had taken a strong liking to Mary's younger sister, Anne.

Despite his dalliances, Henry did not absent himself from his wife's bed, probably more from a desire to produce a legitimate male heir than from a desire for Catherine. In February 1516, Catherine had given birth to a daughter, Mary, who fared better than her other offspring. But though Mary was legally able to inherit the crown, Henry could not invest his hopes in a female, believing that the Tudor claim to the throne was not secure enough to enable a woman to succeed as ruler. There would be dissension; there might even be a civil war if that unprecedented act occurred.

In the fall of 1517 Catherine miscarried. In the fall of 1518 another infant was stillborn. Despite the efforts of her husband, she did not become pregnant again, and by 1527, when she was forty-two, it seemed unlikely that she would provide a male heir for Henry.

Catherine of Aragon had grown matronly. The plump young woman was now stout, her auburn hair had lost its luster, the succession of pregnancies had made her pale and appear older than her years. She gave herself over to religion and attempted to live a life that Falieri, the Venetian ambassador, described simply as "very good." [8]

She could not compete for Henry's affections against the young and vibrant Anne Boleyn, dark-haired, strong-willed, and totally captivating to the king. Like Elizabeth Woodville before her, Anne refused to become a king's mistress. She would be his wife — or nothing. He could not have her as he had had her sister. Her refusal made her only more desirable, and by 1527 Henry had decided that he must have her. She would, he was sure, bear him the son he so ardently craved. She would be his queen.

But to have Anne, Henry must rid himself of Catherine, no easy task. The plan, which seemed so simple when he conceived it, grew into one of international complexity and caused the deaths of some of Henry's loftiest subjects. Catherine would not be calmly set aside, living out her years in a nunnery, as Henry had fatuously imagined. She would be destroyed. Wolsey would be declared guilty of treason; John Fisher would be beheaded, followed by Thomas More. Anne would never have a son, and eventually she too would die by her husband's command.

But disaster and destruction were not in Henry's mind in 1527. He was the paragon of virtue and sincerity as he broke the news to his closest confidants: he had been living in a state of sin for eighteen years. He had had no right to marry Catherine. The papal dispensation that permitted his marriage with his brother's wife had been a fraud. The pope could not contradict the actual holy text, upon which all Church teachings were based. Henry supported his argument on two passages from Leviticus: "Thou shalt not uncover the nakedness of thy brother's wife: it is thy brother's nakedness" (18:16), and "If a man shall take his brother's wife, it is an unclean thing: he hath uncovered his brother's nakedness; they shall be childless" (20:21). Perhaps, offered Henry, Catherine's miscarriages, her stillborn sons, her inability, finally, to conceive were proof of God's wrath against two sinners.

If Leviticus alone spoke against the peculiar situation of one brother marrying another's widow, Henry's case would have been vastly more simple than it was. But opponents to the divorce cited the words of Deuteronomy: "If brethren dwell together, and one of them die, and have no child, the wife of the dead shall not marry without unto a stranger: her husband's brother shall go in unto her, and take her to him to wife, and perform the duty of an husband's brother unto her" (25:5). If Henry's argument was to be based on theology, Deuteronomy would have to be deftly contradicted.

Henry's court was filled with able theologians, Cardinal Wolsey and Bishop Fisher among them. While Wolsey, predictably, wholeheartedly supported the king's move to divorce, Fisher, when asked to comment on the theological basis for the dissolution of the marriage, found Henry's assertions nonsense. He explained that Leviticus referred only to a dead brother's wife with children, Deuteronomy to a dead brother's childless wife. Moreover, all general prohibitions have exceptions, Leviticus included, and should not be taken as absolute and inviolable dicta.

Marriage with a dead brother's wife had been practiced by the Jews, with no detriment to anyone concerned; a man often married his dead wife's sister, an analogous relationship, without condemnation by religious law or by society. Fisher argued further that many precepts of the Bible were outdated for sixteenth-century society and must be re-evaluated. He conclude that the pope had indeed had the right and the ability to dispense permission for Henry to marry Catherine in 1509, and that the marriage was valid then and valid still in 1527.

Fisher, in his apparent naïveté — or perhaps out of loyalty to Catherine, who respected and admired him — believed that he was preventing the dissolution of a happy union.

> With the greatest possible humility of soul [he wrote], I beg the indulgence of the Most Reverend Lord Legates if I now reveal in these written words what I tearfully lament in the depths of my heart. For it makes me tremble even to think of the great inconstancy with which the Apostolic See hereafter will be charged if the Sovereign Pontiff Clement, for a cause which involves no difficulty arising from divine law, should break up a marriage which, in all kindness and all affection, at the solicitation of those most illustrious kings through their ambassadors, he had once confirmed by his authority. O for the misfortune of our times! O for the pitiable ruin hanging over the head of the Church, if there should be such an outcome to this affair — which God forbid! [9]

The conclusion was long in coming. For eight years, Fisher wrote impassioned tracts against the divorce and delivered equally impassioned sermons from his pulpit. He was Catherine's foremost defender, but he could not win against a man in love when that man was Henry VIII.

Henry's letters to his beloved Anne reveal his obsession. He sent her his picture in a bracelet; she returned with a "fair diamond." The majestic ruler groveled before the woman he wanted to marry, "praying you also that if ever before I have in any way done you offence, that you will give me the same absolution that you ask, ensuring you that henceforth my heart shall be dedicate to you alone, greatly desirous that so my body could be as well, as God can bring to pass if it pleaseth Him, whom I entreat once each day for the accomplishment thereof, trusting that at length my prayer will be heard, wishing the time brief, and thinking it but long until we shall see each other again." [10]

If Anne's letters seemed to lack the warmth Henry expected, he was "in great distress, not knowing how to interpret them, whether to my disadvantage, as in some places is shown, or to advantage . . . praying you with all my heart that you will expressly certify me of your whole mind concerning the love between us two." [11]

Henry's hopes for a swift consummation of his divorce and an immediate consummation of his union with Anne were undermined by international politics. Pope Clement VII, who was vital to the unfolding of the drama, was thought to be sympathetic to England because he relied on the country's support against foreign intervention in Italy. But in May 1527, Charles V, with the force of the Holy Roman Empire, sacked Rome and took Clement prisoner. Charles was Catherine's nephew, and Clement's actions, decisions, and policies were suddenly under his control.

Whether or not Clement would side with Henry depended entirely on his choice of political allegiance. It had little to do with theological, moral, or judicial reasons for the divorce. In fact, Clement had recently granted a divorce to Henry's sister Margaret, who had been living in open adultery at the time she asked that her marriage with the earl of Angus be annulled. Margaret, whose first marriage, with James IV, had made her queen of Scots, shocked her brother by her immorality. In a letter, Henry reminded her of "the divine ordinance of inseparable matrimony first institute in Paradise between man and woman." He called the pope's decision a "shameless sentence" and asked her to rethink her actions, not only for her sake but for the sake of her daughter, Margaret Douglas: "The natural love, the tender pity, and motherly kindness towards the fruit of your own body, your most dear child and natural daughter cannot but provoke your Grace unto reconciliation . . ." [12]

The papal judgment, which would allege that James IV was not yet dead — though rumored killed — when Margaret had married Angus, would make her daughter illegitimate, a prospect that horrified the English king. But his own Mary was destined for the same fate if he married Anne Boleyn. He was seemingly unconcerned: Anne, he was sure, would bear a son.

In December 1527, Clement escaped from Charles's imprisonment and was immediately beseeched by Henry's ambassadors for a decision. He was equivocal; then finally, in March 1528, he agreed that Wolsey and Lorenzo Campeggio, cardinal protector of England, could try the case in England. In June 1528 Henry and Catherine were summoned before the court. Henry did not appear for the first session, but Catherine was there, accompanied by John Fisher. At the second session, Henry felt secure enough to appear, and spoke movingly about his reasons for seeking to dissolve his marriage: he could not live any longer in sin; he wanted only justice. Catherine was not deceived. She threw herself on his mercy and that of the court, kneeling before him and begging him to remember their long years of marriage, the grievous deaths of their children, their daughter, Mary, who would be dishonored by the divorce — much the sentiments that Henry had written to his sister. She told the court that their judgment was meaningless. Only by the pope could justice be meted out, and she informed them that she had written to Rome for support. Having said this, she left, and though she was recalled three times, she refused ever again to stand before the court. She was declared contumacious, and Fisher was left to speak not in her name but in her defense.

On June 28, Fisher's mightiest speech against the divorce was delivered to the court. He repeated his contentions that the marriage was valid, and warned the group of the scandals that would result if the divorce was granted. He urged them never to attempt to dissolve the marriage, and promised that, if necessary, he would lay down his life in defense of the holy bond of matrimony that existed between Catherine and Henry. The court was stunned.

The proceedings of the court, Catherine's appeal, and international political pressure all worked on Clement, who by July was ill and spent, wishing for death to end his dilemmas. At last he decided to disband the legatine court in England. He even moved to an alliance with Charles V. He was known to be sympathetic to Catherine and would not yield a decision in Henry's favor. In mid July of 1528, Henry was a despondent man.

He blamed Wolsey. The aide who had supported him, traveled to Rome in his name, taken the burdens of the kingship upon his own shoulders, was repudiated and cast aside. He would be replaced as chancellor by Thomas More, who first refused, and then, under the king's orders, accepted the lofty post.

John Fisher was not deluded into believing that the elevation of his friend to the chancellorship was evidence of some softening of Henry's character. More, thought Fisher, was a man "most brilliant in his character and his intellect and not less outstanding because of his erudition." [13] They agreed on many issues, both political and theological, including the sensitive subject of the divorce. But More could be taciturn. He would be reluctant to assume the authority in which Wolsey had glorified. In fact, Henry wanted just such a man; no longer did he want the chancellor to interfere in his delicate problem.

In 1531 Clement finally issued bulls declaring Henry's marriage to Catherine valid and preventing him from remarrying, on pain of excommunication. Henry could no longer hope to realize his goal diplomatically, and he moved to break, entirely, with the Church in his own land. He returned Anne Boleyn to court, from which she had been discreetly removed for several years, and by late 1532 she was pregnant.

With only months in which to marry her and make his heir legitimate, Henry vested in his own archbishop of Canterbury, Thomas Cranmer, the ecclesiastical authority that had been the pope's alone. Cranmer now could make the final decision about the validity of the marriage to Catherine and the impending marriage to Anne. On January 1, 1533, Henry and Anne were secretly wed. In April, Catherine was informed. By the end of that month, Anne was crowned queen of England. In July, Henry issued a decree depriving Catherine of the right to call herself queen.

> It is therefore evident and manifest that the said Lady Catherine should not from henceforth have or use the name, style, title, or dignity of Queen of this realm, nor be in any wise reputed, taken, accepted, or written by the name of Queen of this realm, but by the name, style, title, and dignity of Princess Dowager, which name she ought to have because she was lawfully and perfectly married and accoupled with the said Prince Arthur . . .
>
> And yet nevertheless the King's most gracious pleasure is that the said Lady Catherine shall be well used, obeyed, and entreated according to her honour and noble parentage, by the name, title, state, and style of Princess Dowager, as well as by all her officers, servants, and ministers as also by others his humble and loving subjects, in all her lawful businesses

and affairs, so it extend not in any wise contrary to this proclamation.[14]

With an arrogance that shocked his countrymen, Henry had achieved all he set out to win. But in September, to the amazement of the court astrologer and to the intense disappointment of the king himself, the long-awaited child proved to be a girl. She was named Elizabeth.

Popular opinion had long been against Henry and his machinations, with rumors and gossip seeding a favorable atmosphere for the rise of a mysterious mystic, Elizabeth-Barton, known throughout the country as the Nun of Kent. From the time she was about twenty, in 1525, Barton had been given to visions and trances, which were said to have been inspired by the Holy Ghost. She was taken up by a monk, Edward Bocking, who saw in Elizabeth the same force that had inspired Joan of Arc and might, he thought, be used to similar ends. Under his guidance, she began to speak not only about religious salvation, but about political matters, including the much-talked-about divorce. For four years, between 1528 and 1532, she was an outspoken defender of Catherine and claimed that if Henry married Anne Boleyn, he would cease to be king within one month. Barton was not dismissed as a madwoman, even by such orthodox theologians as John Fisher and Thomas More.

Henry had no choice but to arrest her, and left her to Thomas Cranmer for judgment. Cranmer conducted repeated examinations, and eventually Elizabeth confessed that she had never had visions, "but all that she ever said was feigned of her own imagination, only to satisfy the minds of those which resorted to her and to obtain worldly praise." In the spring of 1534 she was executed.

Fisher, because of his association with her, was given a small penalty and allowed to go free. But Henry, determined to rid his court of any opposition, saw Fisher as a threat, even with the divorce controversy ended. Henry required all clergymen to support his Act of Succession and Act of Supremacy, giving hereditary rights to his offspring by Anne Boleyn rather than to his daughter Mary, and repudiating the pope as the head of the English Church. Fisher refused. "The Kyng owre soveraign lord is not supreme hed yn erthe of the Cherche of England," he said simply.[15]

Fisher became more than a nuisance; he was a traitor. To the half-dozen bishops who were sent to persuade him to take the required oaths, he replied that they would do better to come over to his side. "Me thinketh it had rather bene all our parts to sticke together in repressinge these violent and unlawfull intrusions and injuries, daily offred to our common mother the holy Church of Christ, then by any manner or perswasions to helpe or sett forward the same . . . The fort is betraid even of them that shoulde have defended yt." [16]

Fisher was deprived of his see of Rochester and, in 1535, imprisoned. In an effort to find incriminating evidence against him, Henry sent a group of commissioners to Fisher's home for a thorough search. The men entered by force, dismissed the servants, and rifled the bishop's goods. They scattered the books from his treasured library, destroying what would have eventually gone to St. John's College. They found some £300 locked in a chest and divided the bounty among them. They discovered Fisher's oratory and greedily broke into a coffer they imagined contained even more gold. Instead, they found a hair shirt and three whips.

Imprisoned in the Tower, Fisher wrote a "Spiritual Consolation" to benefit his half sister, a nun; it was a meditative, somber treatise on the good life. He exchanged letters with his fellow prisoner Thomas More, who, like Fisher, had refused to swear to Henry's oaths and quickly plummeted into disfavor.

Fisher, for his treason, was condemned to a traitor's death:

> You shall be ledd to the place from whence you came [i.e. the Tower] and from thence shall be drawne through the cittie to the place of execution at Tyborne, where your body shall be hanged by the necke: and being half alive, you shall be cutt downe and throwne to the ground, your bowells to be taken out of your body and burnt before you, beinge alive; your head to be smitten of, and your bodie to be devided into four quarters; and after, your head and quarters to be set up where the kinge shall appoint, and god have mercy upon your soule. [17]

But four days after the first sentence was passed, a more lenient writ was handed down, condemning Fisher to death by beheading. He was brought to the scaffold on June 22, 1535. He was said to have met his death calmly and with the same dignity that he had lived his life.

Fisher's head was parboiled, according to custom, and exposed on London Bridge for two weeks. Instead of gradually decaying, it seemed to become more lifelike, healthy, and ruddy with each passing day.

Travelers crossing the bridge were awed by what all took to be a miracle and an ominous portent for the haughty king.

With Fisher dead, the spirit of Margaret Beaufort's life, which he had so faithfully embodied, died too, never to be resurrected by her grandson. But her strength, her passionate determination, her clear-sightedness, and her impeccable standards would one day be revived in her great-granddaughter. When Elizabeth I took the throne as England's Tudor queen, she had learned enough from her family's history to understand the perils to a monarch of both marriage and motherhood. Solitary, on the splendid throne that Margaret Beaufort had secured for her, Elizabeth realized, at last, Margaret's dream and treasured her precious legacy.

Acknowledgments

Notes

Bibliography

Index

Acknowledgments

FOR THEIR assistance in the research for this book, my thanks go to Mrs. P. Basing and the excellent staff of the British Library; the staff of the Houghton Library, Harvard University; Miss H. A. Sherrington of the National Monuments Record, Wales; Sarah Wimbush of the National Portrait Gallery, London; and Mr. Howard M. Nixon, Librarian, Muniment Room and Library, Westminster Abbey.

Special appreciation goes to Frances Apt for her sensitive reading of the manuscript and her unfailing aspiration toward perfection.

Someday, Aaron will know why he was taken to so many libraries and why, when he was very small, he had to share his mother with a typewriter; and I thank him, not least of all, for his sweetness and inspiration.

Notes

CHAPTER I. The Heiress (pages 1–14)

1. Seward, *Hundred Years War*, p. 242.
2. Robbins, *Historical Poems*, p. 185.
3. Cooper, *Memoir of Margaret*, p. 4.
4. Fabre, *Joan of Arc*, pp. 139–140.
5. Ibid., pp. 83–84.
6. Robbins, *Historical Poems*, p. 177.
7. Richard Hall, *Life of Fisher*, p. 139.
8. Ibid., p. 209.
9. Robbins, *Historical Poems*, p. 181.
10. Richard Hall, *Life of Fisher*, pp. 210–211.

CHAPTER II. A Mervaylous Thyng (pages 15–25)

1. Robbins, *Historical Poems*, p. 205.
2. Gairdner, *Paston Letters*, vol. 1, pp. 121–122.
3. Robbins, *Secular Lyrics*, pp. 73–76.
4. Davis, *Paston Letters*, part 2, pp. 35–36.
5. Fisher, *English Works*, p. 293.
6. Graham, *Eternal Eve*, p. 176.
7. Ibid., pp. 146–147.
8. Rowland, *Medieval Woman's Guide to Health*, p. 123.
9. Ibid., p. 125.
10. Graham, *Eternal Eve*, pp. 120–121.

CHAPTER III. Murdre & Much Pride (pages 26–34)

1. Richard Hall, *Life of Fisher*, p. 225.
2. Ibid., p. 208.
3. Robbins, *Historical Poems*, pp. 197–198.
4. Gairdner, *Paston Letters*, vol. 2, p. 297.
5. Gairdner, *Paston Letters*, vol. 3, p. 75.
6. Gairdner, *Paston Letters*, vol. 2, p. 295.
7. Davis, *Paston Letters*, part 2, p. 108.
8. Rosenthal, *Nobles and the Noble Life*, pp. 160–162.
9. Gairdner, *Paston Letters*, vol. 3, pp. 26–27.
10. Rosenthal, *Nobles and the Noble Life*, pp. 160–162.
11. Ibid.
12. Bagley, *Historical Interpretation*, p. 146.
13. Rosenthal, *Nobles and the Noble Life*, pp. 160–162.
14. Robbins, *Historical Poems*, pp. 149–150.

CHAPTER IV. Troublous Times (pages 35–43)

1. Turton, *Builders of England's Glory*, p. 74.
2. Robbins, *Historical Poems*, pp. 210–215.
3. Edward Hall, *Chronicle*, pp. 245–246.
4. Ibid., p. 248.
5. Ibid., p. 250.
6. Gairdner, *Paston Letters*, vol. 3, p. 250.
7. Edward Hall, *Chronicle*, p. 254.
8. More, *The History of King Richard III*, p. 5.
9. Edward Hall, *Chronicle*, p. 254.
10. Robins, *Historical Poems*, p. 218.
11. Ibid.

CHAPTER V. While Lions War (pages 44–53)

1. Comines, *The History of Comines*, vol. 2, p. 49.
2. More, *The History of King Richard III*, p. 62.
3. Edward Hall, *Chronicle*, p. 264.
4. More, *The History of King Richard III*, p. 62.
5. Holinshed, *Chronicles*, p. 284.
6. Edward Hall, *Chronicle*, p. 295.
7. Shakespeare, *Henry VI*, Part 3, Act 4, Scene 6.
8. Edward Hall, *Chronicle*, p. 295.
9. Shakespeare, *Henry VI*, Part 3, Act 2, Scene 5.

CHAPTER VI. The Thorn (pages 54–66)

1. Davis, *Paston Letters*, part 1, p. 440.
2. Davies, *Medieval English Lyrics*, pp. 173–175.
3. Ibid., pp. 191–192.
4. Mancini, *The Usurpation of Richard III*, p. 67.
5. More, *The History of Richard III*, p. 57.
6. Ibid., p. 56.
7. "Memoirs of the Lives of King Edward IV and Jane Shore," p. 14.
8. "The woful lamentation of Jane Shore."
9. Myers, *The Household of Edward IV*, p. 123.
10. Mancini, *The Usurpation of Richard III*, p. 67.
11. Ibid., p. 59.
12. Robbins, *Historical Poems*, p. 111.
13. More, *The History of Richard III*, p. 8.
14. More, *Utopia*, p. 7.
15. Holinshed, *Chronicles*, p. 380.
16. Ibid., p. 381.
17. More, *The History of Richard III*, p. 55.
18. Ibid., p. 42.
19. Ibid., p. 68.
20. Ibid., p. 69.
21. Mancini, *The Usurpation of Richard III*, p. 132n.

CHAPTER VII. The Rebel (pages 67–79)

1. Rawcliffe, *The Staffords*, p. 35.
2. More, *The History of Richard III*, p. 85.
3. Ibid., p. 88.
4. Ibid., pp. 89–90.
5. Chrimes, *Henry VII*, p. 329.
6. "A short view of the long life."
7. Ibid.
8. Ibid.
9. Holinshed, *Chronicles*, p. 414.
10. Pollard, *The Reign of Henry VII*, vol. 1, pp. 4–6.
11. "A short view of the long life."

CHAPTER VIII. Bosworth (pages 80–92)

1. C. R. N. Routh, *They Saw It Happen*, p. 2.
2. Sneyd, *A Relation*, p. 21.
3. Ibid., pp. 20–21.

4. Ibid., p. 24.
5. Davies, *Medieval English Lyrics*, pp. 224–225.
6. Clendening, *Source Book*, p. 77.
7. Rubin, *Medieval English Medicine*, p. 101.
8. Clendening, *Source Book*, p. 77.
9. Ibid., pp. 76–77.
10. Ibid., p. 78.
11. Ibid., p. 79.

12. Hindley, *England in the Age of Caxton*, p. 240.
13. Ibid., p. 241.
14. Gairdner, *Houses of Lancaster and York*, p. 224.
15. Rowse, *Bosworth Field*, p. 254.
16. Comines, *The History of Comines*, vol. 2, p. 52.
17. Ibid., p. 50.

CHAPTER IX. A Cheerful Strain (pages 93–104)

1. Hughes, *Tudor Proclamations*, p. 3.
2. Bullough, *Narrative and Dramatic Sources*, p. 349.
3. "A short view of the long life."
4. Brereton, "The Most Pleasant Song," p. 78.
5. Robbins, *Historical Poems*, p. 148.
6. Ibid., p. 184.
7. Cooper, *Memoir of Margaret*, pp. 35–36.
8. Fuller, *The History of the Worthies*, p. 454.

9. Strickland, *Lives of the Queens*, p. 425.
10. Sneyd, *A Relation*, pp. 97–100.
11. Robbins, *Historical Poems*, p. 95.
12. Strickland, *Lives of the Queens*, p. 427.
13. Edward Hall, *Chronicle*, p. 425.
14. Talbot, *Medicine in Medieval England*, p. 131.
15. Edward Hall, *Chronicle*, p. 426.
16. Cooper, *Memoir of Margaret*, pp. 34–35.
17. Myers, *Household Book*, p. 116.

CHAPTER X. Of Virtue Rare (pages 105–119)

1. Cooper, *Memoir of Margaret*, pp. 97–98.
2. Strickland, *Lives of the Queens*, p. 435.
3. Cooper, *Memoir of Margaret*, pp. 45–46.
4. Ibid., p. 64.
5. Ibid., p. 67.
6. Himes, *Medical History of Contraception*, p. 180.
7. Cooper, *Memoir of Margaret*, p. 18.
8. Reynolds, *Saint John Fisher*, pp. 24–25.
9. Ibid.

10. Robbins, *Historical Poems*, pp. 152–157.
11. Davis, *Paston Letters*, part 2, pp. 484–485, February 10, 1497–1503.
12. Ibid., p. 485; not after April 10, 1504.
13. Robbins, *Historical Poems*, pp. 144–145.
14. Pollard, *The Reign of Henry VII*, vol. 1, p. 160.
15. Ibid.
16. Ibid.
17. Hughes, *Tudor Royal Proclamations*, pp. 12–13.

CHAPTER XI. The House of Mourning (pages 120–130)

1. Davis, *Paston Letters*, part 2, p. 478.
2. Edward Hall, *Chronicle*, p. 493.
3. Ibid., p. 494.
4. Strickland, *Lives of the Queens*, p. 444.

5. More, *The History of King Richard III*, pp. 119–122.
6. Pollard, *The Reign of Henry VII*, vol. 1, pp. 57–58.
7. Ibid., vol. 3, p. 299.
8. Ibid., p. 295.

9. Ibid., pp. 324–325.
10. Ibid., pp. 327–328.
11. Ibid., p. 329.
12. Ibid., pp. 298–299.

13. Ibid., pp. 317–318.
14. Ibid., p. 329.
15. Reynolds, *Saint John Fisher,* p. 25.

CHAPTER XII. The Legacy (pages 131–144)

1. Cooper, *Memoir of Margaret,* p. 132.
2. Ibid., p. 132.
3. Froude, *Divorce,* pp. 32–33.
4. Reynolds, *Saint John Fisher,* pp. 26–27.
5. Surtz, *The Works and Days,* p. 183.
6. Ibid., p. 184.
7. Fisher, *English Works,* p. 291.
8. Froude, *Divorce,* p. 32.
9. Surtz, *The Works and Days,* p. 355.

10. St. Clare Byrne, *The Letters of King Henry VIII,* p. 55.
11. Ibid., pp. 56–57.
12. Ibid., p. 67.
13. Surtz, *The Works and Days,* p. 175.
14. Hughes, *Tudor Royal Proclamations,* pp. 210, 211.
15. Surtz, *The Works and Days,* p. 89.
16. Ibid.
17. Edward Hall, *Chronicle,* p. 119.

Bibliography

MANUSCRIPT SOURCES

The following is among the material in the British Library pertaining to Margaret Beaufort:

Vow of Celibacy, Additional, 5825, f. 224.b.
Her arms, Additional, 584.6, p. 156; 5850, p. 44; 5858, p. 343.
Grant to, by Lord Oxford, Additional, 24,844. f. 58.
Verses addressed to, by Jo. de Giglis, end of fifteenth century. Additional, 33, 772. f. 2b.
Rules for dress of court ladies during mourning, 1502–1503. Additional, 45233, f. 141 b; see also, Stowe, 562, f. 16.
Descents of (handwritten pedigrees), Harley, 1393, 21, 25.
Notice of birth, obituary, etc., fifteenth to sixteenth centuries, Royal, 2A, 18, ff. 30, 30b.
Biographical Notice, Additional, 4244, f. 21.

PUBLISHED SOURCES

Abram, A. *English Life and Manners in the Later Middle Ages.* London: Routledge & Sons, 1913.
Allmand, C. T., ed. *Society at War.* New York: Harper & Row, 1973.
Armstrong, C. A. J. "The Inauguration Ceremonies of the Yorkist Kings and Their Title to the Throne," *Transactions of the Royal Historical Society* (30), 1948.
Aston, Margaret. *The Fifteenth Century: The Prospect of Europe.* New York: Harcourt, Brace & World, 1968.
Bacon, Sir Francis. *History of the Reign of King Henry the Seventh.* Edited by F. J. Levy, New York: Bobbs-Merrill, 1972.
Bagley, J. J. *Historical Interpretation: Sources of English Medieval History, 1066–1540.* Baltimore: Penguin Books, 1965.
Baker, Timothy. *Medieval London.* New York: Praeger, 1970.
Baugh, Albert, ed. *A Literary History of England.* New York: Appleton-Century-Crofts, 1948.
Beith-Halahmi, Esther Yael. *Angell Fayre or Strumpet Lewd: Jane Shore as an Example of Erring Beauty in 16th Century Literature.* Salzburg: Studies in English Literature, 1974.
Berdan, J. M. *Early Tudor Poetry, 1485–1547.* New York: Macmillan, 1920.
Bindoff, S. T. *Tudor England.* Harmondsworth: Penguin Books, 1950, revised, 1978.

Brereton, Humphrey. "The Most Pleasant Song of the Lady Bessie," *Early English Poetry*. Percy Society, vol. 20.

Brown, A. L. "The King's Councillors in Fifteenth-Century England," *Transactions of the Royal Historical Society* (19) 1969.

Bruce, Marie Louise. *The Making of Henry VIII*. New York: Coward, McCann & Geoghegan, 1977.

Bullough, Geoffrey. *Narrative and Dramatic Sources of Shakespeare*, vol. 3 of 8 volumes. London: Routledge and Kegan Paul, 1966.

Burton, Elizabeth. *The Pageant of Early Tudor England, 1485–1558*. New York: Scribner's, 1976.

Calendar of the Close Rolls, 1476–1485, 1485–1500, 1500–1509. London: 1954, 1955, 1963.

Calendar of the Fine Rolls, 1471–1485, 1485–1509. London: 1961, 1962.

Calendar of the Patent Rolls, 1461–1467, 1467–1477, 1476–1485, 1485–1494, 1494–1509. London: 1897, 1900, 1901, 1914, 1916.

Campbell, William, ed. *Materials for a History of the Reign of Henry VII*. Two volumes. London: Rolls Series, 1873–1877.

Cantor, Norman F. *The English*. New York: Simon & Schuster, 1967.

Cavendish, George. *The Life and Death of Cardinal Wolsey*. Edited by R. S. Sylvester and Davis P. Harding, New Haven: Yale University Press, 1962.

Chrimes, S. B. *Henry VII*. Berkeley and Los Angeles: University of California Press, 1972.

———. *Lancastrians, Yorkists and Henry VII*. London: Macmillan, 1964.

———. "The reign of Henry VII," *Fifteenth-Century England, 1399–1509*. Edited by S. B. Chrimes, C. Ross, R. A. Griffiths. Manchester: University of Manchester Press, 1972.

Clendening, Logan. *Source Book of Medical History*. New York: Hoeber, 1942.

Cleugh, James. *Chant Royal, The Life of King Louis XI of France (1423–1483)*. New York: Doubleday, 1970.

Comines, Philippe de. *The History of Comines*, translated by Thomas Danett in 1596. Two volumes. New York: AMS Press, 1967.

Cooper, Charles Henry. *Memoir of Margaret, Countess of Richmond and Derby*. Edited by the Reverend John E. B. Mayor. Cambridge: Deighton Bell & Co., 1874.

———. "The Vow of Widowhood of Margaret, Countess of Richmond and Derby," Cambridge: Cambridge Antiquarian Society (1), 1859.

Costain, Thomas B. *The Last Plantagenets*. New York: Doubleday, 1962.

Coulton, G. G., ed. and trans. *Life in the Middle Ages*, 4 volumes in one. Cambridge: Cambridge University Press, 1954.

Craik, Henry, ed. *English Prose*, vol. 1. New York: Macmillan, 1893.

Cunnington, C. Willett and Phillis. *Handbook of English Medieval Costume*. Boston: Plays, Inc., 1969.

Curry, Walter Clyde. *Chaucer and the Medieval Sciences*. London: George Allen & Unwin, 1960.

Dalgleish, W. Scott. *Medieval England*. London: T. Nelson, 1892.

Davies, R. T., ed. *Medieval English Lyrics*. London: Faber & Faber, 1963.

Davis, Norman, ed. *Paston Letters and Papers*, part 1 and part 2. Oxford: Clarendon Press, 1976.

Denton, Reverend W. *England in the Fifteenth Century*. London: Deighton Bell & Co., 1888.

Bibliography

Dobson, R. B. "Urban Decline in Late Medieval England," *Transactions of the Royal Historical Society* (27), 1977.

Domvile, M. *The King's Mother.* London: Burns & Oates, 1899.

Du Boulay, Francis R. H. *The Age of Ambition: English Society in the Late Middle Ages.* New York: Viking Press, 1970.

Einstein, Lewis. *Tudor Ideals.* New York: Russell & Russell, 1962.

Elton, G. R. *England Under the Tudors.* New York: Putnam's, 1955.

Erlanger, Philippe. *Margaret of Anjou, Queen of England.* Trans. © Flek Books, Ltd. Coral Gables, Florida: University of Miami Press, 1970.

Evans, Howell T. *Wales and the Wars of the Roses.* Cambridge: Cambridge University Press, 1915.

Fabre, Lucien. *Joan of Arc.* Translated by Gerard Hopkins. New York: McGraw-Hill, 1954.

Ferguson, John. *English Diplomacy, 1422–1461.* London: Oxford University Press, 1972.

The First Booke of the Preservation of King Henry the VII when he was but Earle of Richmond, Grandfather to the Queenes majesty. London, 1599.

Fisher, John. *English Works.* Edited by the Reverend John E. B. Mayor. London, 1886; reprinted, 1935.

Fowler, Kenneth, ed. *The Hundred Years War.* London: Macmillan, 1971.

Froissart, Jean. *Chronicles.* Translated and edited by Geoffrey Brereton. New York: Penguin Books, 1978.

Froude, J. A. *The Divorce of Catherine of Aragon.* London: Longmans, Green, 1891.

———. *Life and Letters of Erasmus.* New York: Scribner's, 1894.

Fuller, Thomas. *The History of the Worthies of England.* London: Tegg, 1840.

Gairdner, James. *Henry VII.* London: Macmillan, 1909.

———. *The Historical Collections of a Citizen of London.* Includes: John Page's Poem on the Siege of Rouen, Lydgate's Verses on the Kings of England, William Gregory's Chronicle of London. London: Camden Society, New Series, no. 17, 1876.

———. *History of the Life and Reign of Richard the Third.* Cambridge: Cambridge University Press, 1898.

———. *The Houses of Lancaster and York.* London: Longmans, Green, 1879.

———, ed. *Letters and papers Illustrative of the Reigns of Richard III and Henry VII.* Two volumes. London: Rolls Series, no. 24, 1861–63.

———. *Memorials of King Henry VII.* London: Rolls Series, no. 10, 1858.

———. *The Paston Letters,* 6 volumes. London: Chatto & Windus, 1904.

Gies, Joseph and Frances. *Life in a Medieval Castle.* New York: Crowell, 1974.

Graham, Harvey. *Eternal Eve: The History of Gynaecology and Obstetrics.* New York: Doubleday, 1951.

Green, Alice S. *Town Life in the Fifteenth Century,* vol. 1 of 2 volumes, New York: Macmillan, 1894.

Griffiths, R. A. "Wales and the Marches," *Fifteenth-Century England, 1399–1509.* Edited by S. B. Chrimes, C. Ross, R. A. Griffiths. Manchester: University of Manchester Press, 1972.

Hall, Edward. *Chronicle:* "The Union of the Two Noble and Illustrate Families of Lancastre and Yorke." Edited by H. Ellis. London: J. Johnson, 1809; New York: AMS Press, 1965.

Hall, Richard. *The Life of Fisher,* London: Oxford University Press, 1921.

Halliwell-Phillipps, James Orchard. *Letters of the Kings of England.* Two volumes. London: Colburn, 1846–48.

Halsted, Caroline A. *Life of Margaret, Countess of Richmond.* London: Smith, Elder, 1839.

Hamilton, Franklin. *Challenge for a Throne,* New York: Dial Press, 1967.

Hamilton, William Douglas, ed. *A Chronicle of England During the Reigns of the Tudors by Charles Wriothesley, Windsor Herald.* London: Camden Society, New Series, no. 11, 1875.

Hannon, William B. *The Lady Margaret.* London: Talbot, 1916.

Harriss, G. L. "Cardinal Beaufort — Patriot or Usurer?" *Transactions of the Royal Historical Society* (20), 1970.

Harvey, Nancy Lenz. *Elizabeth of York,* New York: Macmillan, 1973.

Hay, Denys, ed. *The anglica historia of Polydore Vergil.* London: Camden Society, Third Series, no. 74, 1950.

———. *Polydore Vergil.* Oxford: Oxford University Press, 1952.

Himes, Norman E. *Medical History of Contraception.* New York: Schocken, 1970.

Hindley, Geoffrey. *England in the Age of Caxton.* New York: St. Martin's Press, 1979.

Hogrefe, Pearl. *Tudor Women: Commoners and Queens.* Ames: Iowa State University Press, 1975.

Holinshed, Raphael. *Chronicles of England, Scotland and Ireland.* London: J. Johnson, 1807–1808; New York: AMS Press, 1965.

Holzknecht, Karl Julius. *Literary Patronage in the Middle Ages.* London: Cass, 1966.

Houston, Mary G. *Medieval Costume in England and France: The 13th, 14th and 15th Centuries.* London: Adam & Charles Black, 1939.

Hughes, Paul L. and James F. Larkin, eds. *Tudor Royal Proclamations.* Vol. 1 of 3 volumes, New Haven: Yale University Press, 1964.

Hunt, Percival. *Fifteenth Century England.* Pittsburgh: University of Pittsburgh Press, 1962.

Jacob, E. F. *The Fifteenth Century.* Oxford: Clarendon Press, 1961.

"Jane Shore to the Duke of Gloucester." Poem, author unknown, London: Dodsley, 1749. Printed copy at Houghton Library, Harvard University.

Jenkins, Elizabeth. *The Princes in the Tower.* New York: Coward, McCann & Geoghegan, 1978.

Kendall, Paul Murray. *Louis XI.* New York: Norton, 1971.

———. *Richard the Third.* New York: Norton, 1956.

———. *The Yorkist Age.* New York: Norton, 1962.

Kesteven, G. R. *1485: From Plantagenet to Tudor.* London: Chatto & Windus, 1967.

Kittredge, George Lyman. *Witchcraft in Old and New England.* Cambridge: Harvard University Press, 1929.

Lander, J. R. *Conflict and Stability in Fifteenth Century England.* London: Hutchinson, 1969, revised, 1977.

———. *The Wars of the Roses.* London: Secker & Warburg, 1965.

MacGibbon, David. *Elizabeth Woodville, 1437–1492.* London: Arthur Barker, 1938.

Macklem, Michael. *God Have Mercy: The Life of John Fisher of Rochester.* Ottawa: Oberon Press, 1968.

Mancini, Dominic. *The Usurpation of Richard the Third.* Edited by C. A. J. Armstrong, second revised edition. Oxford: Clarendon Press, 1969.

McFarlane, K. B. "England: The Lancastrian Kings, 1399–1461," *Cambridge Medieval History,* vol. 8 of 8 volumes. New York: Macmillan, 1936.

——. *John Wycliffe and the Beginnings of English Nonconformity.* London: The English Universities Press, 1966.

——. *The Nobility of Later Medieval England.* Oxford: Clarendon Press, 1973.

McKisack, May. *The Fourteenth Century: 1307–1399.* Oxford: Oxford University Press, 1959.

McLean, Antonia. *Humanism and the Rise of Science in Tudor England.* New York: Neale Watson Academic Publications, 1972.

Mead, William Edward. *The English Medieval Feast.* New York: Barnes & Noble, 1967.

"Memoirs of the Lives of King Edward IV and Jane Shore." London: E. Curll, 1714.

More, St. Thomas. *The History of King Richard III and Selections from the English and Latin Poems.* Edited by Richard S. Sylvester. New Haven: Yale University Press, 1976.

——. *Utopia.* Translated and edited by H. V. S. Ogden. New York: Appleton-Century-Crofts, 1949.

Mowat, R. B. *The Wars of the Roses, 1377–1471.* New York: Appleton and Co., 1914.

Mullinger, James Bass. *The University of Cambridge,* vol. 1 of 3 volumes. Cambridge: Cambridge University Press, 1911; New York: Johnson Reprint Corp. 1969.

Myers, A. R. *England in the Late Middle Ages.* Harmondsworth: Penguin Books, 1952, revised 1978.

——. *The Household of Edward IV.* Manchester: University of Manchester Press, 1959.

Neaman, Judith S. *Suggestion of the Devil: Insanity in the Middle Ages and the Twentieth Century.* New York: Octagon Books, 1975.

Nivens, J. Birkbeck. *Picture of Wales During the Tudor Period.* Liverpool: Edward Howell, 1893.

Perroy, Edouard. *The Hundred Years War.* New York: Capricorn, 1965.

Pakula, Marvin H. *Heraldry and Armor of the Middle Ages.* New York: A. S. Barnes, 1972.

Partridge, A. C. *Tudor to Augustan English.* London: André Deutsch, 1969.

Pernoud, Regine. *Joan of Arc,* translated by Edward Hyams. New York: Stein and Day, 1966.

Pickthorn, Kenneth W. M. *Early Tudor Government: Henry VII.* Cambridge: Cambridge University Press, 1934; reprinted, New York: Octagon Books, 1967.

Plowden, Alison. *The House of Tudor.* New York: Stein and Day, 1976.

Pollard, Albert F., ed. *The Reign of Henry VII from Contemporary Sources.* Vols. 1 and 3 from three volumes. London: Longmans, Green, 1913, 1914.

Power, Eileen. *Medieval Women.* Edited by M. M. Poston. Cambridge: Cambridge University Press, 1975.

Pugh, T. B. "The Magnates, knights and gentry," *Fifteenth-Century Eng-*

land, 1399–1509. Edited by S. B. Chrimes, C. Ross, R. A. Griffiths, Manchester: University of Manchester Press, 1972.

Rawcliffe, Carole. *The Staffords: Earls of Stafford and Dukes of Buckingham, 1394–1521.* Cambridge: Cambridge University Press, 1978.

Reynolds, E. E. *Saint John Fisher.* New York: Kenedy & Sons, 1955.

Rickert, Edith, ed. *The Babees' Book: Medieval Manners for the Young.* New York: Cooper Square Publishers, 1966.

Riley, Henry Thomas, ed. *Memorials of London and London Life in the XIIIth, XIVth, and XVth Centuries.* London: Longmans, Green, 1868.

Robbins, Rossell Hope, ed. *Historical Poems of the XIVth and XVth Centuries.* New York: Columbia University Press, 1959.

————. *Secular Lyrics of the XIVth and XVth Centuries.* Oxford: Clarendon Press, 1952.

Roderick, A. J., ed. *Wales Through the Ages,* volume 1 of 2 volumes. Llandybie, Carmarthenshire: Davies, 1959.

Roper, William. *The Life of Sir Thomas More.* Edited by R. S. Sylvester and Davis P. Harding, New Haven: Yale University Press, 1962.

Rosenthal, Joel T. *Nobles and the Noble Life, 1295–1500.* New York: Barnes & Noble, 1976.

Ross, Charles. *The Wars of the Roses.* London: Thames and Hudson, 1976.

Routh, C. R. N. *They Saw It Happen.* Oxford: Basil Blackwell, 1956.

Routh, Enid M. C. *Lady Margaret.* London: Oxford University Press, 1924.

Rowland, Beryl. *Medieval Woman's Guide to Health.* Kent, Ohio: Kent State University Press, 1981.

Rowse, A. L. *Bosworth Field.* New York: Doubleday, 1966.

Rubin, Stanley, *Medieval English Medicine.* London: David & Charles, 1974.

St. Clare Byrne, Muriel. *The Letters of King Henry VIII.* New York: Funk & Wagnalls, 1968.

Scarisbrick, J. J. *Henry VIII.* Berkeley: University of California Press, 1968.

Shakespeare, William. *The Riverside Shakespeare.* Boston: Houghton Mifflin, 1974.

"A short view of the long life of that ever wise, valiant, & fortunat commander, Rice ab Thomas," *The Cambrian Register.* London: Williams, 1796.

Seward, Desmond. *The Hundred Years War.* New York: Atheneum, 1978.

Sneyd, Charlotte Augusta, trans. *A Relation, or rather a true account, of the island of England.* London: Camden Society, New Series no. 37, 1847.

Storey, R. L. *The End of the House of Lancaster.* London: Barrie and Rockliff, 1966.

Strickland, Agnes. *Lives of the Queens of England,* vol. 2 of 8 volumes. London: Longman, Green, Longman & Roberts, 1861.

Surtz, Edward, S.J. *The Works and Days of John Fisher.* Cambridge: Harvard University Press, 1967.

Tabor, Margaret Emma. *Four Margarets: the Lady Margaret, Margaret Roper, Margaret Fell, Margaret Godolphin.* London: The Sheldon Press, 1929.

Talbot, C. H. *Medicine in Medieval England.* London: Oldbourne, 1967.

Taylor, Frank and John Roskell, trans. *Gesta Henrici Quinti.* Oxford: Clarendon Press, 1975.

Temperley, Gladys. *Henry VII.* Boston: Houghton Mifflin, 1914.

Thorndike, Lynn. "Magic, Witchcraft, Astrology, and Alchemy," *Cambridge Medieval History,* vol. 8 of 8 volumes. New York: Macmillan, 1936.

Bibliography

Thrupp, Sylvia L. *The Merchant Class of Medieval London, 1300–1500.* Chicago: University of Chicago Press, 1948.

Trevelyan, George M. *England in the Age of Wycliffe.* London: Longmans, Green, 1909.

———. *Illustrated English Social History,* vol. 1 of 3 volumes. London: Longmans, Green, 1949.

Tristram, Philippa. *Figures of Life and Death in Medieval English Literature.* New York: New York University Press, 1976.

Tuchman, Barbara. *A Distant Mirror.* New York: Knopf, 1978.

Tuck, Anthony. *Richard II and the English Nobility.* New York: St. Martin's Press, 1974.

Tucker, M. J. "The Child As Beginning and End: Fifteenth and Sixteenth Century English Childhood," *The History of Childhood.* Edited by Lloyd de Mause. New York: The Psychohistory Press, 1974.

Turton, Godfrey E. *Builders of England's Glory.* New York: Doubleday, 1969.

Vale, M. G. A. "The Last Years of English Gascony, 1451–1453," *Transactions of the Royal Historical Society* (19) 1969.

Vergil, Polydore. *Three Books of English History.* Edited by Sir Henry Ellis. London: Camden Society, Old Series, no. 29, 1844.

Walker, Sue Sheridan. "Widow and Ward: The Feudal Law of Child Custody in Medieval England," *Women in Medieval Society.* Edited by Susan M. Stuard. Philadelphia: University of Pennsylvania Press, 1976.

Wernham, R. B. *Before the Armada: The Emergence of the English Nation, 1485–1588.* New York: Harcourt, Brace & World, 1966.

Williams, C. H. "England: The Yorkist Kings, 1461–1485," *Cambridge Medieval History,* vol. 8 of 8 volumes. New York: Macmillan, 1936.

Williams, Penry. *Life in Tudor England.* New York: Putnam's, 1964.

"The woful lamentation of Jane Shore." Anonymous. n.d., copy at Houghton Library, Harvard University.

Wolffe, B. P. "The Personal Rule of Henry VI," *Fifteenth-Century England, 1399–1509.* Edited by S. B. Chrimes, C. Ross, R. A. Griffiths. Manchester: University of Manchester Press, 1972.

Index

Index

Henry VIII, 125–27, 129, 132, 135–36; coronation of, 130; his determination to marry Anne Boleyn, 136–41; and John Fisher, 142–43
Herbert, Anne, 45
Herbert, William, 44–45, 46, 49
Holinshed, Raphael, 27
Hundred Years War, 1, 2–3, 26

Indenture, 33
Ireland, 37
Isabella of Castile, 117, 121

James IV of Scotland, 117, 118, 120, 139
Joan of Arc, 5–8, 13, 35, 142
John of Gaunt, Duke of Lancaster, 16, 110–11
Jourdemayne, Margery, 9

Lancaster, Duke of. See John of Gaunt, Duke of Lancaster
Landois, Peter, 76–77
Lewis, Edward, 74, 75–76
Linacre, Thomas, 120
Livery and maintenance, 31–33, 117
Lollardry, 111–12, 113
Lomnor, William, 19
London, 42–43, 81–82, 84
Louis XI of France, 46, 48, 49, 50, 55, 57; death of, 76
Love Day, 33–34
Lovell, Thomas, 133
Lucy, Elizabeth, 58, 65
Lydgate, John, 18, 88

Malory, Thomas, 88, 100
Mancini, Dominic, 57–58, 59
Margaret of Anjou, Queen of Henry VI, 31, 32, 56, 74, 96; marriage of, to Henry VI, 13, 26–27; characterized, 27–28; and Wars of the Roses, 39; fleeing of, to Scotland, 42; and Earl of Warwick, 49–50; return of, to England, 51; captured at Tewkesbury, 52–53; death of, 57
Margaret of York, Duchess of Burgundy, 48, 50, 104, 117, 118
Marriage alliances, 75–76, 120–21
Medicine, 101–2
Midwifery, 21–24

More, Thomas, 58, 62–63, 64, 140–41, 142; on murders of Edward V and Richard, Duke of York, 72, 73; death of, 137; imprisonment of, 143
Mortimer, Anne, 16, 19
Mortimer's Cross, battle of (1461), 40, 41
Morton, John, 61, 64, 70, 71, 72, 76; characterized, 62–63; appointed bishop of Ely, 63; and Henry Tudor's invasion of England, 89; crowns Henry VII King of England, 95; becomes archbishop of Canterbury, 98; and James Stanley, 133

Nicholas of the Tower (ship), 18–19
Northampton, battle of (1460), 37

Oxford University, 115, 133

Parron, William, 123
Paston, John, 19, 54, 121
Paston, William, 114
Pembroke Castle, 20–21, 23, 35, 51
Plantagenet, Edward, son of Henry VI, 28, 39
Plantagenet, Richard. See York, Richard Plantagenet, Duke of

Richard, Duke of York, son of Edward IV, 62, 64–65, 71–72
Richard II, 32–33, 38, 95
Richard III, 50, 59, 76, 77–79; characterized, 60–61; his removal of his two nephews, 62–65, 71–73; becomes king, 66; coronation of, 67–69; and Duke of Buckingham, 69–71; his condemnation of Margaret Beaufort, 73–74; and Henry Tudor's invasion of England, 90–91; death of, 91–92, 93
Rivers, Anthony Woodville, Earl, 61–62, 88

St. Albans: first battle of (1455), 30; second battle of (1461), 40–41
St. John's College, Cambridge, 131, 133, 134–35, 143
Sanitation, 84
Shaa, Ralph, 65–66

163

Concerning the type

The text for *Of Virtue Rare* was set in Intertype Baskerville,
modeled after the original designs of John Baskerville (1706–1775),
an Englishman who contributed greatly to the printing industry
as a whole through his work with typography, paper, and ink.
His type is a classic of the transitional style, with generous counters,
a curved vertical stress, and contrast between stem and hairlines.
The display type is handset Garamond, an even older design
based on the sixteenth-century types of Claude Garamond,
a well-known punchcutter and typefounder. The letters are old style,
with smaller counters and wide concave serifs.

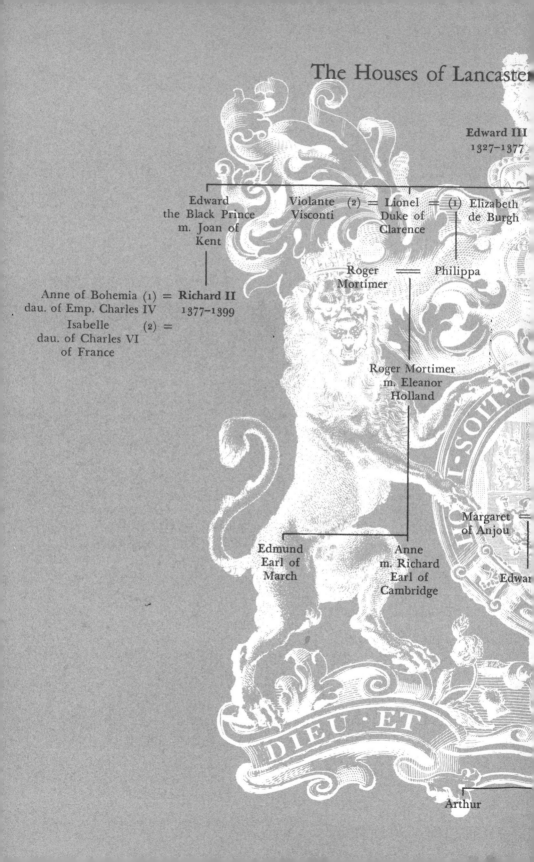

Edward III
1327–1377

Edward
the Black Prince
m. Joan of
Kent

Violante   (2) = Lionel = (1) Elizabeth
Visconti   Duke of   de Burgh
               Clarence

Roger ═══════ Philippa
Mortimer

Anne of Bohemia (1) = Richard II
dau. of Emp. Charles IV   1377–1399
Isabelle   (2) =
dau. of Charles VI
of France

Roger Mortimer
m. Eleanor
Holland

Margaret =
of Anjou

Edmund   Anne
Earl of   m. Richard
March   Earl of
                     Cambridge

Edwar

DIEU · ET

Arthur